CHANGING THE GAME

Praise for
CHANGING THE GAME

The future of our children in sports lies in the hands of parents, coaches, and themselves. This book provides tools and tips to accelerate positive youth development experiences, as well as critical life lessons along the way.

Changing the Game serves as a powerful guide for both parents and coaches who want kids to have fun, enjoyable, and meaningful youth sporting experiences. The 7 Cs section is a must-read for every coach and parent. Many of the lessons and values in this book are timeless and will make a significant impact for everyone involved in youth sports. I highly recommend it!

—**John Ballantine**, president and co-founder,
KIDS in the GAME, www.kitg.org

Changing the Game is, well, a game changer. It explores in both depth and breadth the youth sports experience, its blood, sweat, and tears. Any parent who wants their children to gain the physical, psychological, emotional, and social benefits of what sport has to offer (and isn't that every parent!) better read this book. It will make you a better sports parent, and it will ensure that your children get all the good stuff and avoid most of the bad stuff from participating in sports.

—**Jim Taylor**, Ph.D., author of
Positive Pushing: How to Raise a Successful and Happy Child

Nobody cares more about the integrity of youth sports than John O'Sullivan ... and that is reflected in his great new book, *Changing the Game.*

—**Dan Saferstein**, Ph.D., author of
*Win or Lose: A Guide to Sports Parenting and Strength in You:
A Student-Athlete's Guide to Competition and Life*

I would like to commend John O'Sullivan for this thoughtful and detailed work. I firmly believe that the youth sport experience for a child is shaped as powerfully by their parents or guardians involvement. That involvement by definition is neither a good nor bad thing. Rather the importance of that involvement needs to be appreciated and then it needs to be intelligently managed. In this book John gives practical and helpful guidance to elevating the experience of the children in youth sports by directly addressing the role of the parent or guardian. I think this book helps the ongoing challenge of making youth sports fun and safe as well as somewhere talent can be developed whatever the level.

—**Ian Barker**, Director of Coaching of Education,
National Soccer Coaches Association of America

Changing the Game is full of practical, insightful information that is good for parents and coaches alike.

—**Tim Schulz**, president and CEO, Rush Soccer

Parenting an athlete is not as simple as it used to be. John O'Sullivan has clearly and professionally illuminated this challenging path *with both research and common-sense advice*. This book will help your athlete reach their full potential and allow you to be part of their good memories.

—**Bruce Brown**, founder of Proactive Coaching LLC and author of
Teaching Character through Sport and Proactive Leadership

John O'Sullivan's approach to parenting high-performing athletes is insightful, comprehensive, and effective. He provides practical and relevant principles that can improve communication and understanding between parent and child. His approach helps foster growth and strengthen core family values; most importantly it reminds parents that organized sports is supposed to be fun. *Changing the Game* is a must read for parents who want to take an interactive role in raising confident and well-rounded athletes.

—**Albert Oppedisano**, Psy.D, author of
Education and Empowerment for the 21st Century Parent

As the youth sports landscape has changed over the years, it has left parents oftentimes grasping for air at what to do to help their kids succeed. In my work with younger athletes, it is necessary to devote some of the time to the parents so they can help their kids to improve their mindset, focus, and confidence. As I read John's book, each chapter reminded me specifically of several of my current and former athletes, what they were going through, and their parents' role in the process. *Changing the Game* is a wonderful resource for parents to help their young athletes succeed in sports and life, and I can't recommend it enough

—**Brian Baxter**, director, Sport Psychology Institute Northwest, and author of *The Sports Mindset Gameplan: An Athlete's Guide to Building and Maintaining Confidence*

Changing the Game offers invaluable insights into the reality of the youth sports world and the critical impact that parents have to make or break their kids' experience in sports. John O'Sullivan's thoughtful approach and guidance is spot on and just what we parents and coaches need to help our kids thrive on a field, on a team, and in the game of life!

—**Brian Grossman**, co-founder of KIDS in the GAME

Thank you to John O'Sullivan for providing a wonderful resource to parents of athletes. With such a changing climate of youth sports today, this book provides a guide for parents that brings the focus back on what is truly important for a child participating in sports.

—**Angela Hucles**, two-time Olympic Gold Medalist and founder of the Empowerment Through Sport Leadership Series

Changing the Game should be required for all youth sports parents. This guide offers ways for youth sports organizations to make sure that no child walks around with a hole in their heart. If youth sports organizations implemented this book within their educational efforts we would perhaps see more children involved in athletics beyond the age of fourteen!

—**Vince Ganzberg**, U.S. Soccer National Staff Instructor and co-founder of GK Project

CHANGING THE GAME

The Parent's Guide to Raising Happy,
High-Performing Athletes and
Giving Youth Sports Back to Our Kids

JOHN O'SULLIVAN

New York

CHANGING THE GAME
The Parent's Guide to Raising Happy, High-Performing Athletes and Giving Youth Sports Back to our Kids

Published in New York, New York, by Morgan James Publishing. Morgan James and The Entrepreneurial Publisher are trademarks of Morgan James, LLC. www.MorganJamesPublishing.com

The Morgan James Speakers Group can bring authors to your live event. For more information or to book an event visit The Morgan James Speakers Group at www.TheMorganJamesSpeakersGroup.com.

A **free** eBook edition is available with the purchase of this print book.

CLEARLY PRINT YOUR NAME ABOVE IN UPPER CASE

Instructions to claim your free eBook edition:
1. Download the BitLit app for Android or iOS
2. Write your name in **UPPER CASE** on the line
3. Use the BitLit app to submit a photo
4. Download your eBook to any device

ISBN 978-1-61448-646-6 paperback
ISBN 978-1-61448-647-3 eBook
Library of Congress Control Number:
2013933440

Cover Design by:
Rachel Lopez
www.r2cdesign.com

Interior Design by:
Bonnie Bushman
bonnie@caboodlegraphics.com

In an effort to support local communities, raise awareness and funds, Morgan James Publishing donates a percentage of all book sales for the life of each book to Habitat for Humanity Peninsula and Greater Williamsburg.

Get involved today, visit
www.MorganJamesBuilds.com

Habitat for Humanity®
Peninsula and
Greater Williamsburg
Building Partner

For my wife Lauren,
who helps me to dream big…
For Maggie and TJ,
who encourage me to be a better man…
And for the greatest parents a child
could ever have: my mom and dad.

Contents

| | Foreword | xv |
| | Preface | xvii |

PART I	THE STATE OF YOUTH SPORTS	1
Chapter 1	**The Benefits of Youth Sports**	3
	Shifting the Paradigm in Youth Sports	14
	The Importance of Youth Sports	19
Chapter 2	**The Problems We Face**	23
	Our Values Have Changed	25
	Youth Sports Gone Mad	26
	Money Ball	33
	Chasing the Scholarship Myth	34
Chapter 3	**What Can I Do?**	37
	The Vision of Your Future Child	38
	Match Your Actions with Your Vision	41
	A High-Performing Mindset Is a Happy Mindset	43

| PART II | THE 7 Cs OF A HIGH-PERFORMING STATE OF MIND | 45 |
| Chapter 4 | **The 7 Cs** | 47 |

Chapter 5	**Common Sense**	53
	Keep It in Perspective	54
	Be Patient	61
	Be Grateful, Express Your Gratitude, and Teach Your Child to Do the Same	68
	Matching Your Actions to Your Intentions	72
Chapter 6	**Conditions**	74
	The Factors Determining Athletic Performance	76
	Long-Term Athletic Development (LTAD)	80
	Providing a Safe Environment	94
	Helping Your Child to Learn and Apply Life Lessons	104
Chapter 7	**Communication**	107
	Be an Active Listener	109
	Paraphrase Their Main Points	110
	Respect Their Emotions	110
	Don't Put Your Child on the Defensive	111
	Control Your Emotions	112
	Practice What You Preach	112
	Be Consistent	113
Chapter 8	**Control**	116
	Let Your Kids Go	119
	Setting Goals with Your Child	120
	Start with Three Simple Goals	125
	How to Push Your Child	127
	The Ride Home and the Post-Game Talk	130
	Recognizing if You Have Not Released Your Child	132
Chapter 9	**Competence**	135
	The Definition of Competence	136
	The Games Do Matter but Not How You Think	139
	The Slanty Line Theory	141

Relative Age and the Outlier Effect   142
Overcoming Disappointment   146
Chapter 10   **Confidence**   150
The Definition of Athletic Confidence   152
Where Does Confidence Come From?   152
Game-Changing Question for Parents   154
Allow Them to Fail   154
How to Praise Your Child   158
Chapter 11   **Caring**   164
Love Is Not a Weapon   165
Be Your Child's #1 Fan   166
The Responsibilities of a Sports Parent   174
The Parental Code of Conduct . . .
Written by Your Kids   176

PART III   **CHANGING THE YOUTH
             SPORTS MINDSET**   **181**
Chapter 12   **The Change Begins at Home**   183
Start Small   184
Change Your Club   186
Change Your Country   188

Acknowledgments   193
About the Author   195
Notes   197
Resources and Suggested Reading   201
Helpful Web Resources   203
Sports Parenting Resources   203
**Join the Changing the Game
Project Online**   205

Sport is like a double-edged sword. Swung in the right direction, the sword can have tremendously positive effects, but swung in the wrong direction it can be devastating. The sword is held by adults who supervise children's sports. Whether sport is constructive or destructive in the psychological development of young children greatly depends on the values, education, and skills of those adults.

—Rainer Martens

Foreword

I'M SCARED OF HEIGHTS.

I'm scared of many things actually, but my fear of heights is one of those fears that people don't really get about me. Why? Because I climb mountains.

"Why in the world would you climb mountains if you are afraid of heights?" people ask.

Of course, that is a fair question. I remember leaving high camp on the north face of Mt. Everest as my team was making its final push for the summit. I remember being scared, worried about the technical challenges and the 9,000-foot drops that lay ahead.

What filled my mind much of that night, however, were memories of my childhood: vivid pictures of my favorite hockey coach at the chalkboard, my grandfather cheering from the sidelines, and my mom driving me to countless sports practices. I recalled the values that youth sports engrained in me, such as perseverance, teamwork, and commitment. And now, approaching the summit of Mt. Everest, I realized my moment of truth had arrived. Nearly thirty years after the fabric of my character had been stitched. I would rely on the lessons that sports had taught like never before, if I was to successfully summit the highest mountain in the world.

I climb mountains because I *love* climbing mountains. I love the challenge. I love the teamwork required. I love the cold, crisp air. I love hundreds of things about it. Why would anyone let one fear stop them from doing something they love so much?

Everyone finds themselves in that same dilemma many times during their life. What drives our behavior, fear or love? This is one of life's great challenges, and one we first face as a child—and often playing sports.

Gratitude fills me from head to toe when I think back to all the people that positively shaped my life from a very early age, who taught me to love sports instead of fear them. Now I have a son and a daughter whose mental and emotional fabric is being woven. The thought of *that*—of being largely responsible for the support and guidance of my children—is far more daunting than that terrifying ledge on the top of the world!

The fact that you have this book in your hands tells me that you are in the position to positively shape someone's life right now. In that we share the same opportunity and many of the same challenges. The great news is that this book will help.

Changing the Game offers parents and coaches an invaluable tool to guide the children in their lives. Its approach offers timely advice that is rooted in timeless principles. But it's more than that. It is a call to parents and coaches to improve the entire youth sports environment in order to make sports a more enjoyable experience for our children.

Imagine that a young person in your life asked you, "What is the key to success?" Amidst a host of answers, somewhere in there would be "work hard, study hard, and always be growing."

That is exactly what is required of you to succeed as a tremendous influence in your children's lives now. By taking the time (i.e., doing the work) to read this wonderfully written book and studying the well-researched principles that are presented, you will grow and become much better equipped to handle the challenges and situations that you face in positively leading the children in your life.

I'm cheering both of us on!

—**Eric Plantenberg**, founder, Abundant Living Retreat

Preface

WE ALL LOVE OUR children dearly, and we want to be perfect parents for them. We want sports and school and social activities to be great experiences for them. We want those experiences to reinforce the core values we hold most dear and teach them important life lessons that they can take with them wherever they go. We want our children to be high performers, and we want them to be happy.

But for many of us, when we take our kids to their athletic events, we are not sure that this is happening anymore. Youth sports has changed, and in many ways not for the better.

Changing the Game is a guide to help parents and coaches ensure that athletics is a positive and rewarding experience for our kids. It is also a roadmap for adults to use to give the game back to our kids, to put the "play" back in playing sports.

Changing the Game is more, though. When you buy a TV or a computer or a car, it comes with an owner's manual. This manual tells you what button to push when something goes wrong, how to improve performance, and much more. It ensures that you are never at a loss when it comes to caring for your equipment.

Don't you wish your kids came with an owner's manual?

This guide will help you create your individual "Youth Sports Owner's Manual" for your child. It will help you understand how to help your child build and maintain a high-performing state of mind. This mindset will not only allow him to be a better performer, but it will help ensure that his youth sports experience is an enjoyable one.

This book contains a lot of the material I learned over two decades of coaching and running youth sports organizations. It is supplemented with the latest research about human performance, neuroscience, long-term athletic development, education, and psychology. The data is a compilation of best practices from centers of coaching and education excellence and is backed by science and proven results.

When it comes down to it, though, everything in here pretty much comes from your kids. This is what they would like to tell you about how to make their sports experience a great one. These are the tools you can give them, and the perspective you can maintain, to help them perform their best. This is what they need from you, what they want from you, and how you can deliver it to them.

I hope you will take a few minutes to read the science and the words of performance experts. Most importantly, though, listen to your kids. If you do, the few dollars that you have invested here, and the time you spend reading this, will pay off over and over again. You will be paid back not only in the smiling faces of your kids but through the satisfaction of seeing your young athletes perform their best.

This book will help you build a loving, supportive, and open relationship with your children through sports. It will help you understand what makes your kids tick, how to communicate with them, and how and when to push the right buttons that activate their desire to perform and achieve. It will help you raise your happy, high-performing young athlete and do your part in giving the wonderful world of youth sports back to our kids by first giving it back to your own children.

Enjoy.

PART I

THE STATE OF YOUTH SPORTS

1

The Benefits
of Youth Sports

There isn't any other youth institution that equals sports as a setting in which to develop character. There just isn't. Sports are the perfect setting because character is tested all the time.
—**John Gardner**, Presidential Medal of Freedom winner and founding member of Positive Coaching Alliance's National Advisory Board

The other day as I lay on the sideline soaking up some fall sun and watching my six-year-old daughter's soccer game, I could not help but smile. As the girls laughed and giggled their way up and down the field, trying and failing, falling and getting up, I was witnessing pure joy and exuberance. The parents clapped and cheered, the coaches hustled to keep the ball in play, and everyone involved doled out high fives and cries of "great play" to players on both teams. When my daughter's teammate scored, her teammates all gave her hugs. Then all the girls on the other team gave her a hug. This was youth sports in its quintessential form: pure, unadulterated fun for everyone.

Then I glanced at the field next door, where some ten-year-old boys were playing. As the boys threw themselves about, the parents screamed and yelled to "get up," "get back," "pass it," "shoot it," "hustle!" The coaches screamed at the players, everyone screamed at the referee, and no one was smiling. Unless, of course, there was a goal, at which point the goal scorer would glance to the sideline to see if mom or dad approved. At the same time, the guilty party on the opposing team would put his head down and sulk back to the kickoff while receiving the third degree from his coach and the accompanying groans and moans from the "home fans."

As I sat there, I could not help but wonder: Where did it all go wrong? How did we get from here to there? When and why did we take the joy and romance out of youth sports between the ages of six and ten? Is anyone here watching my daughter's game looking across the way and saying "I want this experience to become like that"? The answer is a resounding no.

This scenario is played out all too often upon many athletic fields, across all sports and all genders. A 2005 study by the University of Notre Dame found that:

- 36 percent of youth reported that coaches yelled at them during a game
- 26 percent of youth reported that coaches urged them to retaliate
- 48 percent of youth reported that coaches yelled at a referee
- 68 percent of youth reported seeing spectators yell at referees
- 43 percent of youth reported being teased by a fan

The innocence and joy of American youth sports has been corrupted. Rarely do kids just get to "play" sports anymore. Instead, they get to "work" sports, a movement caused by the misguided notion that our kids need to specialize early and win at all costs to get that college scholarship and justify the investment made in youth athletics. The romance is gone, the fun is gone, and sports are no longer play.

As a result, 70 percent of young athletes are dropping out of organized sports before they reach high school. Some children quit because of financial hardship, others because they acquire other interests, but many children quit because sports is no longer fun.

After twenty years of coaching elite youth, high school, and college athletes, I have heard almost every kind of query from parents whose children had graduated from "playing" sports to "working" sports. I counseled many parents who felt depressed, helpless, and even defeated by the effect of youth sports on their family. I heard things such as:

- I am so frustrated with my son. He just doesn't seem to care out there anymore. He used to be the best player, and now he just goes through the motions. I have told him that we are taking him off the team if he doesn't start trying harder, and he just says "fine." What should we do?
- The coach won't play my son in his best position, and now he is losing confidence. We need a new coach.
- I want to help my daughter get better, but every time I try to talk to her about sports all she says is "I know, Dad." After games I try to point out the things she needs to do better, but I don't think she is listening.
- Can't you call someone? That other team is so dirty and keeps kicking my son. The referees are so bad that someone is going to get hurt. If you won't make the call, I will.
- This team is not at the level our daughter is. Her teammates are not good enough, and they seem more concerned with having a good time than winning. We know our daughter is good enough to be on the A team. If you won't move her we will find another club.

- She has way too much talent to quit now, and we have invested so much money and time. We are going to see this through, and she is going to play in college.
- My kid isn't starting because there is too much politics on our team.
- My daughter is very talented, and I think she is in line for a scholarship. How can we make sure she gets one so all this money we are spending pays off?
- We never take family trips anymore. Every weekend is filled with games, tournaments, and travel. Our entire life is my kid's sports.

The list goes on and on. How did we get to this point? Over two decades of coaching, I came to realize that there are three main myths held by many parents of young athletes. The belief in these three myths is one of the underlying factors that have caused youth sports to become over-competitive and under-fun.

Myth #1: *Children need to specialize early in a specific sport if they want to play competitively, play high school, play college, or even play professional sports.* The science tells us that this is just not true. With the exception of a few early specialization sports—figure skating and gymnastics as examples—most athletes benefit from a multisport background. Participation in multiple sports leads to better overall athleticism, fewer overuse injuries, and fewer kids who burn out at a young age. Unfortunately, many parents are swayed by travel clubs and private coaches who promise the world, but only if their ten-year-old discards all other activities and dedicates his life to one sport. As we will discuss in our chapter on conditions and long-term athletic development, this is completely false.

Myth #2: *Sports, and especially travel and competitive-level sports, are an investment in a future scholarship or contract.* This myth has been perpetuated by sporting goods companies, beverage makers, and professional coaches looking to make a few extra bucks. A look at the numbers demonstrates that scholarships and pro contracts are reserved for an elite few athletes whose time, effort, and dedication, combined with their talent and a good dose of luck, led them to the higher ground. For the majority of athletes, there is not a scholarship to be had, at least on the playing field. Since 1947, only twenty-three players who participated in the Little League World Series—the ultimate event for twelve-year-old baseball players—have also played in the major leagues. If you are looking at youth sports as an investment strategy, you are just as likely to succeed in paying for college by playing the lottery, and far more likely to succeed by investing the money in a 529 plan. Investing in your child's sport in order to pay for higher education and garner future pro contracts is not a good bet.

Myth #3: *Parents and coaches who want to develop high performers must focus on winning.* The research shows that this is untrue. First of all, while kids like to win, and enjoy winning, it is not why they play. They play to have fun, to be with their friends, to learn, and to wear the "stuff," but they don't play to win. Research has found that parents who try to ensure success often raise unsuccessful kids. Your child has a far greater chance of success if he focuses on preparation, effort, and enjoyment. Your child has a greater likelihood of becoming a high achiever if he strives for excellence instead of championships. Excellence is process-oriented and allows for failure, mistakes, and setbacks. It encourages learning and finding the positives in the performance rather than the outcome. Every child can achieve excellence. Children who focus on excellence are far more likely to be high-performing athletes and ultimately successful ones.

As parents and coaches of young athletes, we spend a great deal of our time and energy focusing on our children's performance. We look at their efforts, their results, and their commitment. We help them to set goals and do our part to help them achieve those goals by taking them to and from training and games, finding good coaches, and buying them equipment. Yet all too often our children "under-perform" according to our expectations, and we are at a loss as to why. There is a simple answer. We do not pay enough attention to their mental state and its effect upon their performance.

Eric Plantenberg lives in my hometown of Bend, Oregon, and by all accounts he is an elite performer both athletically and in the business world. He has climbed to the summit of Mt. Everest, run full Ironman triathlons, and started a school for homeless children in Egypt. He has also been a finalist for *Fortune* magazine's Small Business "Boss of the Year" for his work at his company, Freedom Personal Development. His work focuses on what he calls "The Anatomy of Results."

Plantenberg has immersed himself in the interplay of intentions, state, and actions on performance. He defines *intentions* as a person's vision, goals, and motivation to perform. He defines a person's *state* as "how you show up," the energetic and emotional quality you bring to your activity. Finally, he describes *actions* as "what you do when you show up to perform." What he has found is quite compelling.

Most people believe their actions and intentions have the greatest impact on their results. Plantenberg has discovered through his work with elite athletes, business executives, and others that state of mind is the greatest determinant of high performance. In the most successful people, their intentions and actions account for a portion of their achievement, but their state of mind is responsible for the majority of their success!

When we think about it, this makes a lot of sense. If we use the example of a basketball game, every player on the court likely intends to win the game, wants to play well, and wants to succeed. They all can dribble, pass, shoot, run, and perform the required actions in the game, albeit some better than others. The elite performers are the ones who show up "in the zone," ready to play, and believing in their inevitable success. A talented player who fails to show up in a positive state rarely performs well, while a less skillful player who maintains an abundance of energy and a positive outlook will likely perform his best. Less talented athletes with great attitudes often outperform talented kids with a poor state of mind.

The influence of state of mind on performance has been confirmed through decades of research by world-renowned Stanford University psychologist Carol Dweck. She has discovered that beyond talent, intent, and actions, a person's approach and what she calls "mindset" play a tremendous role in achievement and performance.

Dweck has discovered that people have either a fixed or a growth mindset when it comes to performance. The view a person adopts profoundly affects the way she lives her life, how she performs, and what she accomplishes.

Fixed-mindset individuals believe that their abilities and qualities are carved in stone and that every activity is a test of one's innate, unchangeable ability. Whether it be in the classroom, on the athletic field, or in a relationship, fixed-mindset individuals view every situation as a confirmation of their intelligence, ability, character, and even their personality. Challenges are to be avoided, obstacles are reasons to give up, criticism is ignored, effort is worthless, and the success of others is threatening. Fixed-mindset people do not believe in growth, only validation. You've either got it or you don't!

Here are some things that fixed-mindset people say:

"I don't play much. I am just not a good soccer player."
"I failed the test. I won't ever understand algebra."
"I am not an artist. My brother got all the artistic genes in our family."

Do any of these sound familiar? Do you know anyone whose every failure is a repudiation of his ability? Do you see a player who has potential but is not applying himself? "Why even try?" says the fixed-mindset person. "I am just not good and never can be."

On the other hand, Dweck has discovered that growth-mindset individuals believe that one's abilities are starting points and that talents are capable of being cultivated, nurtured, and developed. Effort, commitment, risk, failure, and disappointment are all components of development and not a reflection of permanent traits. Everything is a part of the journey, and every success or failure is a reflection upon where one is today, not where one might be tomorrow with some effort and application. As a result, challenges are embraced, effort is the path to accomplishment, criticism is helpful, persistence is celebrated, and the success of others is inspiring.

Hopefully we have heard some growth-mindset statements from our kids:

"If I'm going to break into the starting lineup, I need to practice harder and more often."

"I got a C. I need to do some more studying for our next test."

"Wow! That was the most challenging practice we ever had. I like our new coach!"

Growth-mindset individuals love challenges, take risks, try new things, and focus on the process—not the outcome—of achievement activities.

Through her research, Dweck has developed a series of mindset workshops and tested her theories on students of all ages. In one of her studies, she taught a portion of a class a fixed-mindset approach (the brain does not develop, skill is innate and cannot be learned, etc.), while others were led to adopt a growth-mindset approach (this can be learned, ability can be developed). Over eight sessions, both groups of students were taught study skills and how to apply them to learning challenging new concepts. Their teachers were not told which kids were in which group, but they were asked for feedback on student performance.

Throughout the study, teachers singled out far more students in the growth-mindset group for making huge progress in both their motivation and improvement. At semester's end, Dweck looked at the students' grades in math. The growth-mindset group showed an improvement and was far more inspired to learn and put forth effort.

The students in the fixed-mindset group did not improve their grades. In spite of receiving everything the growth group did, except for the growth-mindset training, their motivation to learn and apply their new study skills did not change. Their mindset held them back!

From toddlers to adults, Dweck's results are astounding and consistent. Every study confirmed that the growth-mindset individuals learned more, demonstrated more improvement in testing, challenged themselves more often, and enjoyed themselves more than the fixed-mindset groups. Every time!

The highest-performing athletes are likely to have a growth mindset when it comes to sports. Of course, young athletes and even pros may perform well on a fixed mindset, but they will never reach their true potential. They will constantly seek validation and need to *prove* themselves instead of focusing upon *improving* themselves. In the long run, they will be surpassed by those athletes with a proper growth-oriented state of mind.

The great news is that mindsets can be changed. Dweck has developed workshops and exercises that help students, athletes, and others adopt a growth-oriented mindset. Sometimes it is as simple as watching a short video on how the brain grows and develops throughout life. Other times it is simple statements of praise that have the desired effect. Once people are open to the possibility that nothing is fixed, they can get on with learning and performing their best.[1]

Game-Changing Question for Parents

What mindset do you have? What about your young athlete? Look at the statements below and decide whether you agree or disagree with them (in her book *Mindset*, Dweck uses the word "intelligence," which I have replaced with "athletic ability"):

- Athletic ability cannot be changed much.
- You can develop new skills, but you cannot change your athletic ability.
- Regardless of your level of athletic ability, you can always change it.
- You can drastically change your athletic ability.

If you find yourself agreeing with the first two statements, according to Dweck your mindset reflects a fixed view; agreeing with the last two statements reflects a growth mindset. Give it a try, and make sure your child does as well.

In spite of all the scientific evidence—and I might add common sense —pointing to the importance of mindset, in my experience most youth sports parents and coaches pay little attention to their athletes' state of mind. We tend to spend our time focusing on our kids' intentions and actions. We pay for extra training, buy expensive equipment, and sign them up for the most successful teams, but we forget to communicate openly, share their goals, love them unconditionally, and ensure that they possess a growth mindset. We set our own goals and expectations of high achievement and strive for scholarships and championships. Then we neglect to ask if they are having fun, we ignore the signs of low self-confidence, and we fail to notice the absence of a positive inner voice in our kids. When they don't achieve, our first reaction is often anger or disappointment— "How could this be? I gave you everything you needed and you still didn't win." Yet we didn't give them the most important element of success: a positive state of mind.

A high-performing mindset is a disposition of emotional and mental excellence that allows an athlete to fully utilize his talents, encourages effort, and gives him accountability and control over the learning process.

It requires open communication with parents and coaches, a positive inner voice, confidence, and the knowledge that your love of him is not tied to the outcome of his game. It allows athletes to embrace opportunities and risk, instead of fearing failure.

If your child wants to be a high-performing athlete, he needs to live the lifestyle of a high performer. He needs to have the right goals and intentions and the requisite amount of determination, commitment, and deliberate practice. These things are a given, and every athlete who is pursuing high achievement is capable of performing them.

A high-performing mindset also requires the absence, or at least a minimum, of the physical, emotional, and mental obstructions that many of our young athletes face. These include but are not limited to:

- The pressure to win
- The absence of enjoyment
- Excessive criticism and yelling
- Sports as work and not play
- Poor adult mentors

The list could go on and on, but you get the picture. In order to perform at the apex of their capabilities, athletes need to have certain positive qualities and the absence of negative ones. Our job as parents is to do our utmost to make this happen. When we do, our child can enter a state of high performance.

The best thing about helping your child attain a high-performing mindset: *it does not cost you a penny!* Our youth sports world is filled with $100-per-hour coaches and $300 athletic shoes, all promising to deliver elite performance. While they may certainly help, the single greatest factor that affects performance, your child's state of mind, can be developed absolutely free! All it costs you is time with your kids and a bit of time to learn how to deliver it. It's the best deal going!

Shifting the Paradigm in Youth Sports

Youth sports serve another purpose aside from developing athleticism, one that is far more important for young athletes and will serve them throughout their lives. Sports are the perfect venue to develop character and core values based upon universally accepted social and ethical principles. I am speaking about things such as grit, commitment, integrity, humility, fairness, excellence, and self-control. Sports are a venue to teach kids that failure is a part of learning and that overcoming challenges is a part of life. Youth sports are a microcosm of the challenges, obstacles, and situations our children will face throughout their lives. They are the perfect place to encounter tough teachers and coaches, difficult situations, and events beyond their control. They are a great educational tool. Yet this opportunity is being denied to nearly three out of four American children.

The appearance of the current negative culture of youth sports coincides with the rise of the quick-fix mentality in American culture over the last fifty years or so. We now expect instant solutions that get us in shape, help us lose weight, and make us feel better. From happy pills to diet miracles, our generation now looks outside of ourselves for quick fixes to our problems, our shortcomings, and our issues. We have become a society that lacks accountability for our current situation, and we feel entitled to quick and cost-effective remedies. We are the blameless generation. We no longer recognize that real solutions are only achieved through commitment, effort, and a process that starts from within.

When we think about this as it relates to sports, please recall the scenarios I laid out above. The problem with almost every athlete was "out there," be it teammates, officials, or coaches causing a player's poor performance, lack of commitment, or lack of performance. Parents wanted quick fixes—a new coach, a new team, or new referees—and were certain that all their child's ills would be cured. From time to time, these types of changes could affect a positive short-term outcome, but in the long run these solutions rarely dealt with the root of performance issues, only the symptoms.

If we want to change youth sports in our country, and if we want our children to become athletes who perform to their potential, we need to stop looking for quick fixes and for solutions "outside" of us. We need to look inside ourselves. We need to make a paradigm shift. But what does this mean?

A paradigm shift is an event or action that causes us to see things differently. When we see differently, we think differently, we act differently, and we feel differently. It is a fundamental shift that changes everything, an "aha" moment that changes our attitude, our behavior, and our whole outlook.

One of the greatest paradigm shifts in sports happened on May 6, 1954, when a twenty-five-year-old medical student named Roger Bannister ran the first sub-four-minute mile in history. At the time, it was a widely held belief that the human body was incapable of running a mile in under four minutes. Leading physiologists warned of the dangers to human health for anyone who attempted it. Runners had tried and failed for decades. The general consensus was "It cannot be done."

When Bannister broke the record, a paradigm shift occurred. What was thought impossible was now shown to be possible. Forty-six days later, John Landy ran the second sub-four-minute mile in history, and later that year, in a race dubbed "Mile of the Century," both men broke four minutes in the same race. By 1957, sixteen runners had broken the four-minute barrier. The shift was complete. A new paradigm was in place.

We don't have to run sub-four-minute miles to undergo a paradigm shift. I was once coaching a state playoff game, and my team's top player was having an incredibly poor game. As I got angrier and angrier with her performance and lack of effort, I finally pulled her aside and said, "What's wrong with you? Don't you know this is the playoffs? Don't you even care?" She looked at me and said, "Sorry, coach. I found out on the way here that my grandfather died, and we were very close. My mom is a mess. I just really wanted to try and play today. I know I am letting everyone down. I will try harder."

At this moment, I had a paradigm shift. I viewed my player completely differently. I saw things in a completely new light; I believed differently, I felt differently, and of course I acted differently toward a player who was clearly troubled by things far more important than a game. "I am so sorry," I said. "If you want to play, then go ahead, and just try to enjoy yourself and take your mind off everything. If you don't, that's okay too. It's completely up to you. There are more important things than soccer games."

I felt terrible, but my attitude and behavior were fundamentally different at the end of that short conversation. Nothing changed about the player or her situation. The change was in me. I was able to view her performance through a new lens. I was able to coach her differently, knowing these circumstances. This was a paradigm shift. This is a microcosm of what we need in youth sports.

Over the last two decades, as stories of over-the-top parents, angry coaches, and assaults on officials have become commonplace, we have made efforts to try and change the attitudes and behavior of parents and coaches, but to little or no avail. We have told them to "do this" and "don't do that," but this has had little effect. These adults may have acted differently, but they did so because they were compelled to by league sanctions regarding referee abuse, or rules like "Silent Saturdays" in youth soccer, where no cheering was allowed. The change was only cosmetic and superficial. These changes in attitude and behavior do not get at the root of the issues.

If we want to make real change in youth sports, and real change in our own child's life, we need to see things differently and not just compel people to act differently. We need to define what the true purpose and benefits of youth sports are and recognize why they are so important. We need to recognize where high performance comes from and be accountable for creating environments that allow our children to perform their best. Only then will adult behaviors and attitudes change. We will come to see that change is needed and necessary. This is a paradigm shift. This change starts at home.

The parents of athletes who are both high-performing and happy share a common trait. They have recognized that they cannot change their kids, but that they can change themselves and how they see their kids. They have stopped trying to force their kids to be what they want them to be. Instead they have guided their kids to follow their own path and become what they are capable of becoming. They have opened the door to high achievement and created a positive sports environment. They have shifted their paradigm from "How can I change my kid" to "How can I change so I can be the best parent for my child, and my child can perform his best?"

This is not to say that there are not high-achieving athletes whose parents never recognize this. Of course there are. Their parents never have this "aha" moment where their paradigm shifts. I coached a lot of these kids. The parents pushed their kids relentlessly toward victories, medals, scholarships, and success. Once in a while, these children became very successful and high-achieving athletes. In my experience, though, much of this success came at the expense of family relationships. The child never pursued his goals and dreams, only those of the parent. Many of these kids eventually held the opinion that "If it were not for sports I would not have grown up hating my dad." Numerous famous athletes have written about winning Olympic gold but not being able to celebrate with their mom or dad because sports had ruined that relationship. Achievement at the expense of having a healthy relationship with your family is no achievement at all.

Then there is the 70 percent who drop out of sports by age thirteen. These are the kids who are pushed, prodded, and forced by their parents into situations they want no part of. They never have control, they never become competent or confident, and they stop having fun. Some kids are actually smart enough to see this destroying their family, and they quit before they lose their parents' love and affection. The rest eventually quit, but it's too late, for along with sports went the trust, communication, and unconditional love that is required for a healthy parent-child relationship.

If any of the above scenarios are familiar within your own family, the good news is that you can shift your youth sports paradigm, and it's never too late to do so. This book will share with you the seven principles that parents of happy, high-performing athletes have adopted. I call these the "7 Cs of High Performers."

Making a paradigm shift is a process, not a quick fix. If you are looking for a magic pill, or a solution that allows you to look outside yourself for change, you have come to the wrong place. This is a journey, but it is a worthwhile one. It takes deliberate and sustained action on your part. Along the journey, we will take away the pain, frustration, and disappointment that you might be feeling watching your young athlete struggle and fail. We will replace it with a renewed sense of purpose and a completely different perspective on sports. You will learn how to develop a game plan, an "owner's manual" for your child athlete. This will be your guide throughout his youth sports experience.

You are about to learn the secrets of parents who raise high-performing *and* happy athletes. You will gain a new perspective regarding youth sports. With your renewed perspective, you will be able to raise a child who achieves the maximum performance his ability allows. Most importantly, when her sports career is over, you will have a happy, healthy, and loving relationship with your child.

Beyond this, by embracing and acting upon the seven principles of high performers, you will not only help your own child, but you will begin shifting the paradigm of youth sports. You will join those of us who are allowing our kids to "play" sports again. Together we will take the pressure off of coaches, clubs, and schools to win at all costs. We will allow them to refocus on player and personal development. Once again they will be able to teach the principal core values and lessons that will last a lifetime. We will encourage them to teach excellence instead of success. Perhaps they will win many trophies along the way, but those will ultimately be a result of achieving excellence, and not the outcome of a quest for success. We will give youth sports back to our kids. We will make it fun again, both for our kids and ourselves.

Let's begin our journey.

The Importance of Youth Sports

Off the top of our heads, we can all think of a number of wide-ranging benefits that sports bring to our children's lives. Beyond the physical benefits of improved strength, coordination, flexibility, and overall health, athletics helps our kids understand and adopt healthy lifestyles at an early age. Our kids learn about leadership, communication, accountability, and responsible risk taking. They gain self esteem, determination, and organizational skills. Most importantly, sports should bring fun and enjoyment to their lives.

Youth sports can also bring parents some great benefits. You get to be a part of your child's experiences both on and off the field. You know where they are and that what they are doing is safe, enjoyable, and beneficial to their health. You help them to develop healthy lifestyle and behavior patterns that last a lifetime. From an academic standpoint, studies show that kids involved in sports tend to stay in school longer and get better grades. Sports are a win/win for you and your kids.

Youth sports can provide a safe environment to develop character and learn valuable life lessons that they will carry with them throughout their life. These are traits that will serve them for decades to come and will help them in school, in relationships, in work, and in life.

So what are those lessons? What values are we talking about? In his book *How Children Succeed*, Paul Tough has identified a growing trend in educational theory. This trend is dispelling the notion that IQ is the great determinant in predicting college graduation and life achievement. Instead, he points to a growing body of work that demonstrates a correlation between an abundance of character traits such as grit, curiosity, self-control, and determination with successful outcomes and high achievement. This makes sense. To use the example of a doctor, her intelligence may get her into medical school, but only determination and perseverance will get her through the countless sleepless nights and hundred-hour weeks of residency. Sports can teach our children these traits in abundance.[2]

Raising a child is akin to designing and building your child's long-term infrastructure, as if you were building a house. If you are only building for the short term, you are not worried about things like the foundation, wall strength, or ceiling beams—only first impressions and curb appeal. But if you are building it to last for seventy years, you want a sturdy foundation, strong walls, and a well-built roof. We need to think of parenthood in the same way.

If we are building a solid emotional and moral foundation for our children, we must think long-term. We must think beyond single games or three-month seasons. We must focus not on wins and losses but on core values and principles we want our kids to take from sports. When we think about the long haul, we realize that the purpose of youth sports is not only to develop better athletes but better people. Sports help children build the foundation for becoming a quality adult both on and off the field. Children form their self-image through what they hear said to them and about them. We need to make sure the messages they receive enhance one of the values above, or other values that are important. We need to make sure they are in an environment where these things are not only taught but exemplified by the coaches, the teachers, and the adults charged with educating them.

Trophies, medals, wins, and losses have their place in the youth sport experience, but they are far from the be-all and end-all reasons for kids to play sports. They might be a possible outcome of things like hard work, perseverance, and dedication, but they are the result of preparation and not the reason for it. Many parents and coaches judge the athletic educational process solely by tournament victories, league finish, and final scores. This misdirected focus is harmful not only for a child's long-term athletic development, but it usually places a great strain on a parent's relationship with his kids. As a result, children end up competing more than they practice. They develop poor habits and begin to see your love for them, and belief in them, as tied to wins and losses instead of effort and commitment to the process.

According to the University of Notre Dame's Center for Ethical Education, research shows that kids play sports for the following reasons:

- To have fun (always #1)
- To do something I am good at
- To improve my skills
- To get exercise and stay in shape
- To be part of a team
- The excitement of competition

They do not play to win. They like to win, they enjoy competing, but they do not play to win. They play to have fun, to be with their friends, to feel good about themselves, and because it is exciting. Yet how often do we pick and choose our kids' sports team because it is the winning team, the winning coach, the defending champion, and assume that because of all the wins everything else just happens? We look at wins and losses and fail to search for happy faces and proper developmental environments.

According to Dan Gould at the Michigan State University Institute for the Study of Youth Sports, kids want to have fun, to get better, and to be with their friends. They want parental support and encouragement. They want you to watch them play and praise them for their effort. They want you to be realistic about their ability. They want you to be present and interested in what they are doing. This is the path to high performance. Yelling at their coach, the officials, and them is not. Being overly critical and putting extreme pressure on them is not. They want the game to be theirs![3]

When I ask my former players what their fondest youth sports memory is, it nearly always has to do with a trip we took, a funny incident that happened, or just a team with great relationships. If they mention winning a state title or a big tournament, they usually qualify that remark with something such as "I just love this team so much because it makes winning fun." These players were highly competitive youth soccer players, many of whom have gone on to play in college. The last high-level youth girls' team I coached had thirteen players go on to play college soccer—seven of them to play NCAA Division I—and the team also won four Oregon Youth Soccer State Cup Championships. Yet all of their fondest memories had to do with relationships, van rides, and team trips. It's not that they didn't like winning; they loved it. But their biggest takeaways were the lessons they learned and the friendships they made.

As parents, I believe that whenever possible we should do our best to give our kids what they need and some of the things they want as well. One thing that all kids want, and we are capable of giving them, is a pleasurable sports experience. Better yet, this is the most likely path to high performance for it develops athletes who control their destiny, fall in love with their sport, and as a result willingly put in the time, effort, and commitment needed to perform at their highest possible level.

2

The Problems We Face

Do you know what my favorite part of the game is? The opportunity to play.

—**Mike Singletary**, NFL Hall of Famer

t's hard to venture out to any youth sports field these days and not think *there is something wrong with this picture*. Youth sports do not look like they did twenty or thirty years ago. Sure, there were a few over-the-top parents and coaches, but for the most part kids still "played" sports. It was fun. Children were fearless. There were no cameras streaming ten-year-old baseball games live online. There weren't any high school basketball coaches lining up for the signature of the next great middle school recruit or online statistics of the local youth soccer league. And we certainly did not watch commercials telling us that we need $300 soccer shoes and $400 baseball bats if we hoped to compete next weekend. Things have changed, not only in sports but throughout our culture.

One of the biggest changes is the massive increase in sedentary, non-athletic lifestyles in our country. Among the contributing factors to the decrease in activity is the staggering number of kids who drop out of sports at a young age. As mentioned, an incredible 70 percent of kids drop out of organized athletics by age thirteen. Some drop due to financial constraints, others due to time constraints, but most stop playing because it just isn't fun anymore. The people responsible for this, and the only ones who can change it, are the adults.

We face quite a few challenges if we plan on trying to move the bar and get the adults out of our kids' games. Youth sports are a multibillion-dollar industry now, with many corporations, hotels, small businesses, and even entire cities dependent upon the youth sports industry. The entities competing for players and their dollars have driven up the price and the stakes of youth sports. The corporations that provide athletic opportunities, run events, and sell equipment count on sports to improve their bottom line.

Parents, often against their better judgment, feel compelled to keep up and are made to feel guilty if they do not. Many believe they will cost their child a college scholarship, or a shot at the pros, unless they buy the latest bat or hire the special skill coach. The adults and their over-involvement in the kids' games have shifted the entire paradigm.

The fact that so many kids are quitting sports by age thirteen has created a generation of inactive adults. As a result, the obesity epidemic is one of the greatest, if not the greatest, challenges facing our country today. Obesity-related conditions include heart disease, stroke, diabetes, and certain types of cancer, and the epidemic is sweeping our country. According to April 2012 Statistics from the Centers for Disease Control and Prevention, more than one-third of U.S. adults are now obese (35.7 percent), and not a single state in our country has met the 2010 goals of reducing obesity to below 15 percent. Obesity-related health care spending was $147 billion in

2008 and grows every year. The cause of obesity: poor dietary habits and lack of activity.[4]

But this is only the tip of the iceberg.

Our Values Have Changed

Youth sports might be our last great hope to teach and maintain the traditional American values of perseverance, humility, integrity, compassion, courage, and the like. Our schools are struggling to do it. The Internet is not doing it. And popular culture is certainly not doing it.

Our culture has changed radically in the last decade. Kids are bombarded from all sides by pop culture values that older generations were rarely confronted with. Those values are leaching onto professional sports as well, and some might say youth athletics is not far behind. The message kids are receiving is not the one I want my kids to hear, and I imagine most of you would agree. Perseverance has been replaced by instant gratification, humility has been supplanted by a quest for fame, and respect has been displaced by "what's in it for me?"

A 2011 study by UCLA psychologists Yalda Uhls and Patricia Greenfield examined television data over the past fifty years. Their study demonstrated that the values expressed by the shows most popular with kids ages nine to eleven have changed drastically during that time. From 1967 through 1997, shows such as *The Andy Griffith Show, Laverne and Shirley, Growing Pains,* and *Sabrina the Teenage Witch* dominated the ratings in this demographic. The values represented by the shows changed very little during that period. The five most expressed values were community feeling, benevolence, image, tradition, and popularity, while the five least expressed values were fame, physical fitness, hedonism, spiritualism, and financial success.

Fast forward to 2007, and the most popular shows, *American Idol* and *Hannah Montana,* exemplify the new top five values of fame, achievement, popularity, image, and financial success, closely followed by self-centeredness, ambition, conceitedness, and materialism. The bottom five values are spiritualism, tradition, security, conformity, and benevolence. The emergence and prevalence of new technology, such as computers, mobile Internet, and hundreds of television channels, can be all encompassing and always present. It has given popular culture a new level of influence upon our children's lives.[5]

Today, many of the shows aimed at our nine- to eleven-year-olds are about children who are seeking fame through the entertainment industry. As a result, as one study found, fame has become the number one value that children ages nine to eleven aspire to. Another study found that being famous, attractive, and rich topped the list of the most important things for children under age ten. The result, says psychologist and parenting expert Dr Jim Taylor, is that "these distorted values are definitely not going to prepare [kids] for life in adulthood where, for most of us, narcissism and aspirations of wealth and fame don't usually play well with reality."[6]

Youth Sports Gone Mad

I was the executive director of Oregon Rush Soccer Club in Bend, Oregon, from 2006-2012. During that time I had the pleasure of coaching many excellent players, among them Joseph "Miguel" Martin. Miguel's story provides an extreme example of the overwhelming nature of American youth sports.

When he was fourteen, Miguel's schedule with Oregon Rush consisted of a fall and spring season, some summer events, and either the winter off or some additional winter skill training. This in itself was quite the burden for the family, who happened to live forty minutes from his team's practice facility. His mother is a well-known artist and his father a successful horse breeder with plenty on their plates already. Nevertheless, Miguel was a passionate, energetic boy who loved the sport of soccer, and his family supported his dreams.

Miguel was also one of the eighteen best players in his age in Oregon and was selected to the Oregon Youth Soccer Olympic Development

Program (ODP), adding additional training on ten weekends throughout the winter and spring, two to three additional weekends away for ODP events, and a weeklong United States Region IV identification camp in July. This made soccer a bit more of a burden, but Miguel loved the game and he was pretty darn good at it.

Actually, Miguel was not only pretty good but very good, and he was identified as one of the top players not only in Oregon but in all of U.S. Youth Soccer Region IV, which encompasses fourteen western states stretching from Colorado to Hawaii, Arizona to Washington. As a result, Miguel was invited to an extra week of Regional Holdover camp. There he was identified as one of the top goalkeepers in the region, and he was invited to an additional week of Region IV events. Phew, Miguel was running out of weekends.

Miguel was then identified as one of the top fourteen-year-olds in the United States and was invited to a weeklong United States Soccer Federation National Team Camp. What an honor for Miguel and his family, who were incredibly grateful to their coaches and teammates for helping him achieve this high honor. Of course they attended that event in Massachusetts. And there went Miguel's last few holiday weekends of the year, never mind most of the family vacation time and money (his family has had to write a check for every club season and event, state team fees and camp fees, regional camp fees, and at times travel to regional team events! Thank God the national team at least covered his travel and expenses).

But wait, there's more. Because Miguel was identified by U.S. Youth Soccer and the United States Soccer Federation as a top player in his age group, another entity, U.S. Club Soccer, invited him to one of its ID2 Player Development Camps. If he performed well there, he had the potential to be invited to the National ID2 Camp with the best fourteen-year-olds in the country. These were all fantastic opportunities: additional weeks with great players and some fantastic free gear from Nike. All he had to do was pay for his flights and the rest was covered. Okay, his family said, we can swing this too, because if Miguel did well there he might get to go to Spain or Argentina on the…you guessed it…all-expenses-paid U.S. Club Soccer ID2 international trip!

Now, before you say "Wow, that is too much to ask of a kid," let me warn you that we are not even close to done. Back in Miguel's hometown, his Oregon Rush club team did pretty well and was a finalist in the U.S. Youth Soccer Oregon State Cup Championships. If they won, they got the right to represent Oregon at the U.S. Youth Soccer Far West Regional Championships, and here comes another week away in Arizona, California, Idaho, or perhaps even Hawaii. If they won that one, then it would be time to head off to the U.S. Youth Soccer National Championships. That means another week on the road and more flights and hotels to pay for.

But they did not win the Oregon State Championship. Well, that was okay because they could still attend the U.S. Club Soccer Regional Championships in Seattle, and if they won that they could go to the U.S. Club Soccer National Championships. Or they could go to the Super Y League National Championships if they chose to play in that league. Or they could even go to U.S. Youth Soccer Presidents Cup regionals and nationals if they played those events.

On top of all this, Miguel and his talented teammates on the 1997 Oregon State Team could win the ODP Region IV Championships and head off to ODP National Championships. Or perhaps Miguel would be lucky enough to be invited to the Nike Manchester United Cup North American Championships in Portland, Oregon, where the winner gets an all-expense-paid trip from Nike to the Manchester United Cup World Championships in England.

Our fourteen-year-old soccer players in the United States can compete in five separate events that each crown a national champion! It almost boggles the mind. But wait. I'm not finished.

After a crazy summer, Miguel was done with regionals and nationals, club and ODP, and was looking forward to a few days of rest.

Unfortunately, it was time for…high school soccer! That's right, Miguel was a talented freshman, and the varsity coach was salivating at the chance to call up his promising young goalkeeper. Miguel's national team camp, the culmination of an entire year of hard-core soccer, finished just two days before the beginning of pre-season fitness training. Instead of some good rest and recovery, Miguel now needed to earn his way onto varsity by putting his tired body through a grueling week of two-a-day fitness sessions. Then he had three more months of five-day-a-week soccer that could have led to a state championship!

Unfortunately, his team didn't make the state final this year—but even if they had, he would have missed it because he needed to fly to Florida to play with the U.S. Youth Soccer Region IV team at their interregional event. And then the cycle started all over again.

Does this seem right to you? Miguel is a great player with wonderful, supportive parents. He loves soccer, and his parents have not pushed him into any of these things. He has aspirations of college and professional soccer, and he is capable of achieving those dreams. The problem is that even when everything is right in Miguel's situation, the system has made the environment an overwhelming one. Miguel is doing fine, but many kids in his shoes burn out and quit. You can see why.

The story of Miguel is real and is happening all across the United States every year in many sports. With each team and each event, Miguel was often exposed to great coaches, incredibly talented teammates, and great competition. In my experience, at these levels in soccer, the coaches are amazing and well-meaning, and they really have the best interests of the kids in mind. The kids participate in high-level training and learning environments. Every one of these programs on its own would be an incredible experience for a young athlete. But taken together, the sum is not greater than its parts. The experience is diminished.

One of the biggest challenges we face in our youth sports landscape is the sheer volume of playing opportunities that exist for our kids, as evidenced in Miguel's situation. This may not exactly sound like a problem, but later on when we discuss the need for proper training periodization, tapering, and recovery for young athletes, you will see how all these choices are actually hurting performance rather than developing high-performing athletes.

Twenty to thirty years ago, kids usually played in local recreational leagues, followed by some school ball. High school sports were usually the highest level of competition available to a young athlete, and making varsity was most everyone's goal regardless of sport. A few town teams would travel to an event or two, and of course Little League has its regional and national world series.

According to Rick Wolff in his 2003 book *The Sports Parenting Edge*, this began to change in the 1980s when some adult soccer players decided they wanted to extend their kids' soccer seasons beyond the fall. The success of these travel leagues and events, coupled with the accelerated player development of young soccer players, led to a movement to create travel leagues for baseball, basketball, hockey, volleyball, and other sports. Today, most communities have at least one travel team in a variety of sports, beginning as early as age seven or eight and lasting through high school.[7]

Aside from the logistical and financial challenges travel sports place on families, they place very difficult burdens upon the young athletes. Not only do they make it more challenging to be a multi-sport athlete, but for the best players, selection to additional all-star teams, state select teams, and even regional and national events can become an incredible time drain and detrimental to their health.

This problem exists in U.S. youth soccer because there is no integration of the competing entities under one development scheme. Schools, clubs, ODP programs, travel programs, and the like are competing business entities with bottom lines to meet. They have their own seasons, their own championships, their own schedules, and their own agendas, which often overlap. Instead of training and peaking for specific competitions throughout the year, and then recovering appropriately, kids go from one "most important week of the summer" with their club to a second "most important week" with ODP to a third, a fourth, and on and on. They never rest, they never peak, they never recover, and they try to maintain a high level week after week, month after month. It is not physiologically possible to do this. Pros cannot and will not do it, but we expect growing kids to. Because do not forget, Miguel was in the middle of his growth spurt! My knees hurt just thinking about it.

Some parents tell me that when they were kids, they played all the time and their kids can too. They are right to an extent. We did play all the time, not distracted by video games, six hundred TV channels, and computers. But we played for fun and not under the watch of our parents or adult supervisors each and every day. We did not go from playing under one sports microscope to another, being evaluated week after week, being put to the test day after day. We just played in the park, on the street, on the pond, and away from the spotlight of adult judgment. When we succeeded we smiled, and when we had a bad day we smiled, because we were with our friends, it was fun, and the results did not really matter.

Some sport governing bodies are doing their best to at least put the elite players on a more sensible track. This is a great start, but even these organizations are getting some pushback. The United States Soccer Federation, for one, has recently mandated that its elite U16 and U18 boys in the U.S. Developmental Academy program (USDA) no longer play high school soccer. The reason behind this is to establish a nationwide, ten-month season that puts over eighty clubs on the same national schedule. It mandates specific requirements for training versus competition ratios and gives players adequate rest and recovery. These are the elite fifteen- to eighteen-year-old male soccer players in the United States.

This requirement from the USDA does not cover the vast majority of potential boys' high school soccer players in the United States, yet the pushback has been immense. Articles have been written in many of the nation's biggest newspapers, school coaches have complained, and clubs have been denied the use of school facilities, all because the USDA has decided to place its elite players in a program and on a schedule that is backed by the latest science in athletic development. This program provides them with proper periodization, rest and recovery, and mandates skill development. Yet we still have two separate entities competing for the same customers, and thus it is a national news story.

Whether I agree or disagree with the USDA decisions is a moot point, as I can see both sides. The point is to illustrate what happens even when various entities start doing everything correctly from a scientific, child-centered perspective. Their competitors still exist and may be very vocal in their opposition and quest for paying "customers." High schools make an excellent point that for some kids their high school soccer experience is a great one, as they get to represent their school and play in front of their friends. I completely agree, as do many former high school players who are now professionals.

That said, I also agree with U.S. Soccer that the current system where players like Miguel are "developed" is not educating players properly and is not serving the kids. I agree with them that putting the best players in a single ten-month program where they can potentially receive higher-level coaching and competition (as opposed to seven months of USDA and three months of high school soccer) will in the end produce better soccer players. I think someday there will be a happy middle ground, but right now it's one or the other, and they are both right. It is a really tough choice for kids, but one that the best science in athletic development says they should make.

The soccer example illustrates the problems caused by non-integration in youth sports, but it would be foolish to think the same issues do not exist in baseball, volleyball, basketball, hockey, and other sports. As long as there is a scarce commodity (players) and competing suppliers (schools, clubs, select teams, etc.) basic economics tells us there is going to be competition for the scarce dollars that belong to the players and the families. And that leads us to our next big challenge to American youth sports: MONEY.

Money Ball

An astronomical amount of money is being spent on youth sports by parents, as well as huge investments by corporations who profit off of equipment, tournaments, recruiting services, and even live streaming Little League games. This has created among parents a "keep up with the Joneses mentality" in everything from Little League to youth soccer. Unwary adults are told their kid needs to be on the travel teams by age seven, have a private coach by eight, and be committed to a single sport by age ten.

This long-term involvement in competitive travel sports may in turn yield years of large financial commitments. By the teenage years, many parents say "Look how much we have spent on your sports! You are going to play in college!" This focus upon the "investment," and the return on that investment in the form of a scholarship, obscures the main reasons why our children participate in sports. The fun is gone and replaced by work. Learning life lessons and teaching character become secondary to playing in front of college coaches and earning a scholarship. The true purpose of sport is lost.

In his 2012 book *The Most Expensive Game in Town*, journalist Mark Hyman describes how youth athletics has stopped being solely about the kids. Hyman concludes that it is now driven by adults who make a living off of youth sports, and the parents who are spending tens of thousands of dollars on the latest equipment, the best camps, and the best coaching. Hyman asserts that our youth sports setup perpetuates the myth that all our kids are going to be college or professional athletes if they just buy the $400 bat, the $250 soccer shoes, attend just one more camp, or hire that private coach. This incessant message is bought into by vulnerable parents, who are buying everything from DVDs that teach physical literacy to six-month-olds to thousand-dollar recruiting services promising exposure to hundreds of college coaches.[8]

The current adult-centered youth sports environment reaches kids of all ages and abilities. I was recently looking for new soccer cleats for my five-year-old son and was stunned to find that there are $120 soccer shoes that come in size 1. Another company streams Little League baseball games live via a backstop camera so all the moms and dads can watch even if they cannot make it home from work. I wonder, did anyone ask the kids if they wanted to be on display like that?

In researching this book, I asked both Hyman and Dr. Jim Taylor whether they thought this situation would ever be changed by the corporations and business leaders in youth sports. They were unequivocal in their answers. "No, there is too much money involved now. This needs to be a bottom-up solution," said Hyman. "Parents need to realize that their job as a youth sports parent is to help their kid be the best athlete he can be and receive the lifelong values that sports can teach, not a scholarship. Parents need to take a hard look and see that what we are doing in youth sports, and what we are doing to our kids, is wrong and has to change."

Taylor agreed. "The challenge is that those running sports now have incredible power and set the agenda. Parents are adapting to that environment. It's time for them to make some tough decisions about what they value most, and make sure youth sports delivers those values."

Chasing the Scholarship Myth

Why are parents supporting the status quo and accepting the poor state of youth sports? Unfortunately, it is because far too many parents believe that this is the only path to a collegiate sports scholarship. They are chasing the scholarship dream.

I hate to be the bearer of bad news, but chances are small that your child is going to play a college sport, even smaller that he will receive a scholarship, and miniscule that he will be turning pro. I know that every commercial you have seen has told them to "Just do it," and every special camp, coach, or piece of equipment you have purchased has promised to be the difference between star and also-ran, but it's just not true. Your children should dream big, and they must have lofty aspirations. As the adult, you need to provide perspective. If your goal in enrolling your kids in sports is to get a scholarship, you are setting them, and yourself, up for a high probability of failure.

The sad statistics indicate that while only 3-5 percent of high school athletes even play in college, an even smaller number receive athletic financial aid. About one in one thousand high school athletes receives a college scholarship (most of them only partial), and about one in thirteen thousand ever becomes a professional. Unfortunately, even in the face of those numbers, between 30-50 percent of youth sports parents believe their child is good enough to get a scholarship. This reality distortion is one of the effects of a youth sports culture that promises the latest bat, the newest shoe, or the most elite camp will have college coaches knocking down your door with a big check in hand.

Take this one step further. Even if your child gets a scholarship, outside of football and basketball the average scholarship is less than $10,000, meaning it only covers a portion of the $20,000 to $60,000 a year of school costs these days. Consider that number against the $5,000 to $10,000 a year you are investing in your kid's youth sports teams. At every College Night presentation I ever did, I told the audience that if you want a guaranteed way to pay for college, take your youth sports money and put it in a 529 college savings plan, because chances were that was only way your current sports investment was going to pay for school (although given the recent performance of my kids' 529s I may have to reconsider this example).

There are not enough scholarships to go around. There are also a plethora of fantastic schools your athlete should consider (Ivy League, Patriot League, all of NCAA Division III) that don't even give scholarships, but offer amazing athletic and academic programs. Are you really going to strike all these schools off your kid's list because they don't have athletic scholarships? Youth sports can be about a lot of things, and getting a scholarship can happen for a small percentage of youth athletes, but it should not be the primary reason to play. Unfortunately, the entire economy of youth sports has shifted the message from "Play to have fun and be an athlete for life" to "Play hard and get a financial return on my investment." We need to shift it back.

Throughout my career, I have worked with athletes and parents from every type of sports background. While there is no exact profile of a positive, supportive sports parent, some of the easiest parents to work with have been former professional and elite amateur athletes. Why? First, they have fulfilled their sports dreams and do not expect their kids to fulfill them. Next, they understand the hours of training, the weekends away, and made the massive commitment needed to become an elite athlete. They know how hard it is, how dedicated one must be, and how you need not only talent and commitment but a few breaks along that way. While they may have high aspirations for their child, they have already accepted the fact that it is very unlikely their kids will be able to do what they have done because it is incredibly difficult to do. This is perspective, something we will speak a lot about in Part II of the book.

3

What Can I Do?

So many of our dreams seem impossible, then improbable, then inevitable.

— **Christopher Reeve**

I f we are going to move the bar and change the culture of youth sports, we must not be naïve about the challenges we are facing, both on and off the field. The status quo is well funded, entrenched, and has convinced many parents to accept the new reality of youth sports. Their products may be fantastic and give great value to players and families. The products are not the problem, nor are the people behind them. It is the culture in general, and we all bear some responsibility for that unless we do something to change it. We need to shift the paradigm.

Throughout the rest of this book, I am going to give you a series of Action Steps that will help you make positive changes in your child's youth athletic experience and begin changing the game in American youth sports. I will also provide you with questions to ask your child so that you may begin the discussion about the role of sports in his or her life. These questions will help you determine your child's state of mind when it comes to sports and identify ways to help them improve it.

Here is your first action step. Think about what you want your children to get out of youth sports. This will give you a vision of your child five, ten, even twenty years in the future. It will give you a sense of direction and a sense of purpose behind all of your sports-related decisions. Here's how.

The Vision of Your Future Child

I recently had a conversation with a parent about his sixteen-year-old daughter. She is a talented soccer player on a very good team. For years she struggled with her self-confidence, as she possessed an inner voice that told her she was not good enough. One day her parents made the decision that if she was going to get one thing out of sports, it would be self-confidence. With that goal in mind, they changed their focus from wins and losses and began to judge her progress based upon whether she was growing in confidence. They provided their daughter not only with excellent coaching but the support and tools needed to help her become a confident athlete. They formed a vision of a confident young woman taking to the field each and every game, ready to face whatever challenges confronted her.

This player was recently at a high-level regional championship event, and she was playing against an incredibly talented and fast forward whom she was having trouble marking and keeping pace with. Twice she was beaten, the second time costing her team a goal in a crucial game. "At this point a year ago, she would have packed it in, asked for a substitution, and come up with an ailment or a reason to come out of the game," her dad told me. But not this time.

"I saw a different look in her eyes and in her posture," he said. "She got a little tactical advice from her coach, nodded her head, and her whole demeanor said, 'That is not going to happen again.' She was not beaten for the rest of the game, and her team went on to win the game.

"She will take that moment with her the rest of her life," her father said proudly. "She can fall back on that June day in Arizona, in 113-degree heat, as a day when she decided to take a stand and grow up, to believe in herself. She became a young woman before our eyes. That moment was worth every practice, every disappointment, everything she went through as a player to get there. And no one can ever take that away from her."

It all started with a vision!

You are the architect of your child's future, and your dreams for them are the plans from which you will construct their future. They are the basis for every action you take and every investment you make on your child's behalf. You can design and build whatever you want, and you are limited only by what you create in your mind. That is not to say the vision cannot change, or that there will not be bumps in the road. As long as you know where you are going, though, you will find a way to get there.

It is hard to produce a result that is bigger than your vision, so you better think big. This goes for everything you do in your life, but especially when it comes to your vision for your children. Try not to sell them short by envisioning medals and state titles. Imagine them at twenty-five, at thirty-five, at fifty-five, being incredible human beings, loving spouses, and great parents. Act every day to get them there. Go out and act to make your vision a reality!

As Christopher Reeve says, at first this grand vision will seem impossibly far away, but then we see the vision becoming reality. It seems improbable, as our child becomes a young adult, and we start to see important adult qualities emerge in his personality, his character, and his demeanor. Finally it becomes inevitable. Our child becomes a strong, confident adult. Could there be a prouder moment as a parent?

I have never met a parent who dreams about his child growing up to be lazy or dishonest or a failure. No parent envisions a future for his child that is not prosperous or filled with opportunity, abundance, and loving relationships. Every parent I have ever met wants their son or daughter to possess things like courage, integrity, sportsmanship, humility, and passion. They all intend for their children to achieve greatness in their lives.

But what do we do to get them there? Let's be like an architect and design a plan. Let's think for a moment what your son or daughter might look like as a high school graduate, as a college graduate, as a parent. Is he or she strong, confident, and charismatic? Is he or she humble, yet bold and enthusiastic? Does he or she get along well with others, face challenges with an "I'll try" instead of an "I can't" attitude?

Think about your core values, the things in life that are most important to you and your family. If someone were to describe you or your family to a stranger, they would say "The Jones family is _____, _____, and _____." Do not limit yourself to three things; list as many as you like. Figure out what is most important, what you stand for beyond all else.

Now, make an effort to visualize your child in twenty years, or perhaps forty years. Please complete each of these exercises for yourself; write them down and put them in a safe place where you can refer to them from time to time:

- List the core values that you want your child to possess as an adult.
- List the life lessons that you would like your child to learn from sports.
- Envision your child as an adult, possessing these values, these strengths, looking you in the face, smiling. Picture graduation from high school or college. Picture their wedding day. See your child in the future.

You now have a vision of your child. Sear that image into your mind. This vision you have formed will be your plan, your architectural rendering, of your child as an adult. Everything you do from here on out will have a single purpose: to ensure this vision becomes a reality. Everything.

Now ask yourself one simple question.

Are my actions today leading to this future person, or leading to something entirely different?

Match Your Actions with Your Vision

It is crucial that from this point forward your actions in life match your vision when it comes to your child. Whatever you intend your child to become, whatever you dream she might accomplish, whatever your goals are for her they must be complemented by your daily actions.

This seems like a simple concept, but every day in youth sports tens of thousands of well-intentioned parents act in a way that is detrimental to their child's athletic development and overall growth. I am not speaking about assaulting coaches and referees or beating up other parents. These things are aberrations, and no one would argue that they have any value or place in sport. I am speaking about the subtle things we sometimes do as parents, such as yelling instructions from the sideline, criticizing coaches and teammates, or focusing on wins instead of development. These are the actions that are well intentioned yet are a hindrance to high performance.

I have never met a single parent or coach who intentionally stunted a child's development or set out to make sports a miserable experience. Their intentions were usually great. Unfortunately, I have met countless numbers of parents and coaches whose actions do nothing but hinder the physical, mental, and emotional development of the kids they are charged with developing. They invest thousands of dollars on equipment, coaching, and travel, but not a second is spared to think about where they are going and whether anything they are doing is actually helping. Many have never even asked their child what he or she wants!

Raising a child that matches your future vision is kind of like the game of Concentration from our childhood. You remember it? You matched two-of-a-kind pictures on a board, and once you did those pieces began to reveal a hidden image. If the pictures did not match, you lost your turn. You kept matching the pictures until more of the hidden image was revealed and you could finally solve the puzzle.

What you are doing from this point forward is the same thing as Concentration, only the image that is being revealed is that of your future child. When one piece of the puzzle (your action) matches a second (your vision), you win and your vision is partially revealed. When they do not match, you lose your turn, or in this case, it does not lead to the future child. The more your actions and vision match, the more pieces are revealed, and soon the vision begins to take shape.

We will be faced with many choices throughout our lives when it comes to our children. We will be forced to distinguish whether our children's sports, schools, activities, and friends are congruent with our values or with the empty values espoused by popular culture. We will ask ourselves whether the major influences in our kids' lives develop character and teach the lessons we want them to learn, or instead hinder this development. We will be forced to choose whether to follow and fight for our values or allow pop culture's values to win. This choice can often be a difficult one—unless you have a vision of where you are going. Know your destination, and then focus on the journey!

Forming a vision and a plan is one of the most critical exercises you will ever do for your young athlete. I encourage you to take some time with this and go through the easy steps I have outlined below. This vision will become the cornerstone for all decisions you make from here on. Have fun with it. Years from now, you will look back and be amazed at how important this was.

A High-Performing Mindset Is a Happy Mindset

The beautiful thing about forming your vision and setting out to build a high-performing, growth-oriented mindset in your young athlete is that this type of mindset also leads to greater enjoyment for your child. Enjoyment does not only come from winning as some parents believe; it comes from having control, gaining competence, and having a sense of purpose through participation in sports. To have these things, they need flow.

In the 1970s, famed University of Chicago psychologist Mihaly Csikszentmihalyi coined the term "flow" to describe a previously unacknowledged mental state of performance and satisfaction. In flow, people have clear goals and a perfect balance between what they have to do and what they are capable of doing. They are challenged, which serves to focus attention and prevent boredom. Yet they are not challenged in an excessive way, which would create anxiety. In flow, a person's body and mind are stretched in a way that increases focus and makes effort a satisfying reward. They are so deeply involved in the moment, and in control of their experience, that time and place melt away, leaving them in the zone of high performance.

Our children naturally exist in a state of flow; they learn from us to "grow" out of it! Children live moment to moment, seeking competence, filled with joy and purpose. They perform their best because they are always fully engaged in the moment. Unfortunately, we encourage them to evolve out of this state, to grow up, even though science tells us that they will perform better when they have flow.[9]

Children who possess a high-performing, growth-oriented mindset are far more likely to achieve a state of flow—and thus happiness—in their sports experiences. In Part II, I will give you the tools to encourage flow in your young athletes and help them develop a high-performing state of mind.

Action Steps for Forming Your Vision

1. Define the core values that are most important to you and that you want to see in your child.

2. List the life lessons you hope your child will learn from athletics.

3. Form a vision of your future child.

4. Ask yourself: are my actions leading toward my vision, or something entirely different?

PART II

THE 7 Cs OF A HIGH-PERFORMING STATE OF MIND

4

The 7 Cs

In Part I we outlined the problems in youth sports and discussed the changes in our societal values that present additional obstacles to a positive sports experience. We began defining our vision of our child, a critical foundation for navigating the journey through childhood. In Part II we jump into the real nuts and bolts of raising a high-performing athlete and in the process making their youth sports experience an incredible one.

To start, here are a few of the main questions and issues that many parents expressed to me over the years:

- I have no idea what my kid is supposed to be learning at this age, or what it even means to be a good athlete.
- My kid doesn't seem to care about sports anymore, and he won't even talk to me about it.
- My daughter is so lacking in confidence that she doesn't want to play anymore; she says it's not fun.

47

- I try to help, but when I talk about it on the ride home after games, my son just rolls his eyes at me.
- I've invested so much time and money, and my kid doesn't even care about sports anymore. What do I do?
- We haven't taken a family trip in years that hasn't been for sports.

Any of these sound familiar? If so, you are certainly not alone. Every parent of a young athlete has encountered these questions, or ones just like them. Raising children is not black and white, nor is it a straight journey to a predetermined destination. We want to do our best for our kids and give them the greatest chance for achievement. Yet it can be so frustrating and confusing at times.

Part II of this book will lay out a plan to help you navigate that path toward creating a high-performance state of mind in your young athlete. As we discussed in the first chapter of the book, most people believe that their actions and intentions have the greatest impact on their results. This may be the case for average performers, but not so for those who are above average, whether it be in sports, business, or any other achievement type activity. State of mind is the greatest determinant of high achievement.

In my experience coaches rarely put an adequate amount of attention on their athletes' mental state, and neither do parents. Most of our time and energy is spent focusing on the actions our players take, and to some extent their goals and intentions. This is not to say that we should ignore training, games, fitness, and the like. It is to say that we need to pay more attention to how our athletes show up to these activities. What is their attitude toward their sport? What are they motivated by? Are they confident or afraid to fail? In a nutshell, what is their state of mind with regards to their sport?

Ask any coach for the reason his team played poorly and the answer is almost always "we just were not into it today," "we were afraid of that other team today," or something similar. They have prepared, they have the skill, they hope to win, but they do not show up in the right frame of mind to be successful, to work hard, or to give their best effort. This is not an intention thing. This is not an action issue. This is all about how the athletes "showed up" to play.

Parents and coaches have a huge influence on their athletes' state of mind when it comes to sports, school, or any other activity. By understanding the components of a positive state, you can help your athletes shift their whole attitude and approach to sports. Once you understand the components of state, you will likely shift your own approach toward their participation in and preparation for sports. You may recognize some actions and behaviors from your past that you thought were helpful, and that you undertook with only good intentions, yet were actually detrimental to your child's performance. I know I did, and once I recognized the need to change these things, I saw a dramatic performance increase in my athletes. I am confident that within these pages you will find similar things to help your own child.

To begin, we must have an understanding and acceptance of what I call the 7 Cs of a High-Performing State of Mind. The 7 Cs are the most basic components of environment, motivation, communication, and perspective that every child needs to approach their activity with a positive outlook, enjoy what they are doing, and perform at their highest level. Adults are responsible for helping to create this positive state by providing our children with:

Common Sense: In other words, have some perspective and see the big picture. Have a vision. Be the adult. Be patient and understand that sports—like school—require a long and difficult educational process. Be grateful for all the positives that sports bring to your life, and express that gratitude. Allow your children to fail, and be there to remind them of the lessons. Be the parent that your child needs in their life to keep it all in perspective.

Conditions: Children need a sports environment that is physically, mentally, and emotionally safe, as well as developmentally and philosophically appropriate.

Communication: The basis of any positive parent/child and coach/child relationship is good communication. There are some basic principles of communication that will help you have a more open and constructive relationship with your child.

Control: Give your kids age-appropriate control in decision making. As your kids mature, you will be ceding more control over their decisions to them, but that does not mean you cannot start when they are young. Notice what your seven-year-old likes and then help him or her choose a sport. As your kids grow older, get to know what their goals are and learn to accept them. Teach them about commitment, but let them go seek their own sports destiny. Give them ownership of their successes, and help them understand that successful people are also the ones who fail most often.

Competence: Children learn best when they see the results of their hard work. You will learn how to ensure your child feels competent and capable as they learn a new sport or progress to a new level in a current one. Education is a process that requires trial and error, failure and success, so allow your children to fail, and be patient as they learn.

Confidence: Acquiring skill helps a child become confident, and confident children pursue their interests with more vigor, authority, and passion than children who do not believe in themselves. Learn how your actions (and inactions) can help your child become a confident athlete.

Caring: Kids need unconditional love. A child must never think that your love for them is conditional and based upon performance in sports. Your love must be unconditional, and your words, your actions, and your emotions must reflect your love no matter the situation before you. Become your child's #1 fan.

The 7 Cs work in conjunction with each other, and improving one area perpetuates improvement in others. For example, giving your child *control* helps them become more *competent*. Gaining skill leads to greater *confidence*. That in turn encourages your child to take more *control*, and the cycle continues. Here is a look at how the 7 Cs work:

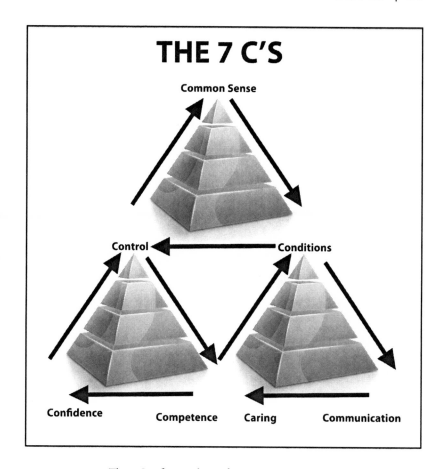

The 7Cs of a High-Performing State of Mind

By the same token, if you do not help your child in one of the seven areas, enjoyment can disappear and development slows. For example, if your child is in a poor environment, and you are unable to communicate with them about it, then the whole experience starts to crumble. You cannot show them your caring and unconditional love. As a result, the environment continues to deteriorate.

As we navigate through the 7 Cs, at the end of each chapter I will give you some concrete Action Steps to help you implement each of the 7 Cs, as well as some discussion points and questions to ask yourself and your young athlete. Through these steps, and conversations with your kid, you will gain some great new insight into your child, and some of the answers may even surprise you. Most importantly, this dialogue will help you see where your child's approach to sports may be healthy, and which areas may be lacking and need work. Let's get started.

5

Common Sense

Live with intention. Walk to the edge. Listen hard. Practice wellness. Play with abandon. Laugh. Choose with no regret. Appreciate your friends. Continue to learn. Do what you love. Live as if this is all there is.

—Mary Anne Radmacher

H ave a plan, challenge yourself, play hard, have fun, be bold, make friends, always learn, love what you do, and just do it. This is what children can learn from sports each and every day, and what keeps them in a great frame of mind. This is also what far too many children never learn because they leave sports at a young age, disillusioned with athletics and our sports culture.

If you have enrolled your children in sports to teach them character, you must keep sports and life in their proper perspective. Children play sports because it is *play*, and they quit when it becomes work. "We don't stop playing because we grow old, we grow old because we stop playing," said George Bernard Shaw. If you do nothing else as a sports parent, make sure your kids never stop playing. This is what I call *common sense*, and there are four main components:

1. Keeping perspective
2. Practicing patience
3. Expressing gratitude
4. Matching your intentions to your actions

Keep It in Perspective

In order to keep the proper perspective, you need to first remind yourself of the reasons why kids play sports. They are:

- To have fun (always #1)
- To do something I am good at
- To improve my skills
- To get exercise and stay in shape
- To be part of a team
- Excitement of competition

Kids do not join sports, or stay in sports, to win. They play because sports are fun, because they are *play*, and they drop out when they stop being fun. As golfing great Jack Nicklaus says, "You have to love a sport to play it well, and love grows out of enjoyment."

When I run down this list in my workshops, I often get the comment "My kid is a travel/all-star player. This survey sounds like answers from a bunch of recreational kids." Dr. Dan Freigang, a well-known sports psychologist who works with the national team athletes from U.S. Soccer, USA Hockey, and the U.S. Ski Team, got this question often as well. As a result, he conducted the same survey with the elite youth and professional soccer, hockey, and ski team members. The results? Exactly the same!

The elite athletes that Freigang works with play for the exact same reasons as all kids do. Their job may be to win, and their focus may be on attaining results on an international level, but they are still motivated by the joy and camaraderie that participation in sports brings them. If your child is an elite-level player, chances are the reasons for playing listed above apply to her as well.

As mentioned in Part I, statistics provided by the National Collegiate Athletics Association (NCAA) demonstrate that only one in one thousand youth sports participants ever becomes a collegiate scholarship athlete, yet surveys that show 30-50 percent of parents believe that their children have a good chance to play at the college level or beyond. This lack of perspective can become potentially damaging to a young athlete and to the relationship between the child and his parents.

To be blunt, if you do not possess perspective and common sense, you need to seriously consider whether you should enroll your child in sports or for that matter any other activity where achievement is measured. If you do not have perspective, you are likely setting your child up for failure, and setting yourself up to be disappointed in your child. You will likely place undue burdens and expectations upon your kids, demanding more than they are capable of or willing to provide. With unrealistic expectations, you are more likely to become frustrated with your child's performance and blame her or her coach for failing to develop and showcase her talents. Unless you know why you are enrolling them in sports, what you expect from the experience, and what the potential positives and negatives are, then you need to take a step back and reassess.

In his book *Positive Pushing*, Dr. Jim Taylor outlines a very healthy and grounded approach to athletics that parents can take. He urges parents to adopt the following perspective:

"The primary purpose of my child's participation in [sports] is to gain its life lessons and psychological, emotional, social [and physical] benefits including, but not limited to, fun, love and mastery of an activity, motivation, commitment, confidence, focus, emotional maturity, ability to handle competition and pressure, responsibility, discipline, cooperation, leadership, teamwork, and time management, which will benefit my child later in life. Anything else—for example, great success, fame and fortune—is just icing on the cake."[10]

This chapter will help you to ask the right questions, and make sure you are keeping sports in their proper perspective. At the end, you will be asked to come up with a family mission statement about the purpose and benefits of sports for your child. With perspective and a common-sense approach to youth sports, it will probably look something like Dr. Taylor's statement above.

Understand Your Coach and Help
Your Coach Understand Your Child

The University of Notre Dame Center for Ethical Education has developed a thorough resource for coaches, administrators, and parents called the "Play Like a Champion Today Educational Series." PLC is a collection of research and educational tools designed to teach sports as ministry. They have some excellent material on the relationship between parents and coaches, as well as training for coaches on how to communicate better with parents to explain their role and what the relationship should look like. Here are some of their suggestions.

The Parent's Role: It is important to understand that while the role of a parent is to look out for your own child above all else, the role of a coach is to look after all children under his care. Most parent-coach conflicts arise out of a misunderstanding of these two positions. Coaches sometimes think parents are asking for special treatment, and parents believe that coaches are not being responsive to the needs of their child. This usually arises out of a lack of communication.

It is up to parents to have an open dialogue with coaches and help them understand your perspective. Let them know about any special needs or situations that involve your child. If you are aware of something that may be affecting your child's approach, perhaps a death in the family, a team personality issue, or even a lack of understanding about the coach's expectations, let your coach know!

If you communicate your child's needs, your child's struggles, and how she is responding to a coach, most coaches will change how they talk to your child when they realize that what they are currently doing is not working. A coach may have fifteen to twenty players on his team and only see them three to four hours a week, so it is very difficult to gauge how every kid is responding to you in the short term. As a parent, let them know in a respectful manner, and take away all the guesswork.

The Coach's Role: Coaches are responsible for letting you know their perspective on coaching the team. If they are not forthcoming, as a parent you should ask them. Coaches should help you understand that they must be sensitive to the needs of the entire team, not just a few individuals, and that every child cannot be praised, coddled, or coached at every moment (nor do they want to be!).

Coaches should provide a preseason letter of introduction. It's also a good idea to hold a team meeting, at which they let you know their philosophy and their mission and provide boundaries and guidelines that govern proper and improper communication, behavior, and the parent-coach relationship. When I ran large youth soccer clubs, nearly every issue I ran into with unhappy or confused parents arose out of a coach's failure to have this meeting and get everyone on the same page.

With my own teams, before I had this parent meeting I would ask the players to define their goals and ambitions for the season and compile that information so I could let the parents know what their kids wanted. I would then do my best to let everyone know where I was coming from in terms of player commitment, training, team goals, my coaching philosophy, and expectations for them as parents (i.e., being good fans, modeling sideline behavior, commitment, etc.) I also assured them that I was always available for a phone call or via email or in person to discuss any larger issues that might be arising with their child. I was not there to discuss someone else's child (unless it involved illegal or unethical behavior), just their own.

Over the years I had many meetings relating to playing in college, drug and alcohol use, education and grades, performance and behavior, and yes, parenting of young athletes. I never shut my door on a parent, and I never turned down a conversation or a meeting. At times we had to agree to disagree, but I believe the parents of the kids I coached would acknowledge that I always gave them a chance to speak their mind, and I was not afraid to tell them the truth. I believe that all coaches should follow a model of openness and integrity. Many coaches fear that this is additional work; I assure them that it actually saves you work in the long run.

Balance Sports and Life

Perspective also requires keeping a balance between sports and other aspects of family life, such as school, church, social life, family trips, and your relationships with your other kids and spouse. Athletics can provide you a front row seat to your child's growth and development, but it can also become a divisive wedge between the athlete who gets a lot of attention and siblings who might fade into the background. Kids are acutely aware of how mom and dad divvy up attention, praise, and time, and they may become jealous and less confident if their dreams and ambitions play second fiddle to a star athlete.

Help all your kids to understand that they have unique gifts and abilities, and try to impress upon them that you are aware of these gifts. Help each of them find their path, be it in sports, music, art, or wherever their heart leads. Make sure they know that their passions are just as important as their siblings'. If need be, keep a log of the time you spend with each child, and take notice if your athlete is getting a lot more of your time than your non-athletes are. If this is the case, you may need to block out additional time for your other kids so no one feels left out.

Youth sports can create heavy demands upon your time and finances, and these need to be kept in balance with overall family needs. You might be trading family dinners for practices, church for games, and vacations for coaches' fees and equipment. It is important that as a family you decide what your priorities are and what you want out of your children's sport experiences. If you want to grow closer as a family, there are ways you can use sports to do that. But don't be afraid to draw the line and say "Enough! We are taking our family vacation this year." If you value family dinners, do not schedule activities for every night of the week, and make sure that some nights are "family date night." When you keep everything in perspective, it helps your kids see the big picture as well.[11]

Remember that your kids may be the most important thing in your life, but they are not the only important thing. It is easy, and tempting, to put aside everything that we love to do for the sake of our kids and their activities, but this is not a very healthy way to live. It sends your children the message that the world exists to serve them, and it does not. If the annual family camping trip is very important to you, do not cancel it. If Friday night family dinners are a cornerstone of your family unit, then make them happen. Make time for yourself to work out and play sports, make time for spiritual growth, and make time for you and your spouse to catch up and unwind every day.

This does not tell your kids you do not love them. On the contrary, it shows them that they are a beautiful and unique part of a highly complex and integrated world, which at times will focus its attention upon them and at other times push aside their interests and opinions. This is life, and it is important that we demonstrate this for our children. Sure they may not like it and tell you "It's not fair." But as my son is fond of telling his older sister, "It's not no fair, Maggie. It's yes fair."

Finally, take heart from these additional words from Dr. Jim Taylor, which I believe sum it all up nicely:

> If your objective is to turn them into champions, the odds are that you're wasting your money and time and your children's happiness. Sports are metaphorically littered with the scarred psyches of children whose parents tried and failed to do what Earl Woods and Richard Williams succeeded at doing. Your goals as parents are for your children to have fun, learn life skills to succeed later in life, value health and fitness, and develop a love of sports. If by some freak chance you give them world-class athletic genes, they love the sport enough to work incredibly hard, they get the right kind of support from you, and they become professional or Olympic athletes, then that's just icing on the cake.[12]

Without perspective, it is difficult to find safe and developmentally appropriate conditions for your child and then give them control. It is hard to communicate and show caring and unconditional love. It is hard to raise children who are confident. Without perspective, you cannot be the adult in the relationship, for being an adult entails having life experience and a big-picture view on each and every situation you encounter.

On the other hand, with perspective and common sense you will be in a position to support and encourage your child to be a high performer. You will allow him to gain the benefits of his chosen activity that will serve him throughout his life. You will be able to do this while maintaining a healthy balance between athletics and family life, and also while developing a positive relationship with your child. You will be aware of your child's state of mind and approach to sports. You will be well on your way to raising a high-performing athlete.

Action Steps for Keeping Perspective

1. Remember why kids play sports...to HAVE FUN!
2. Develop a partnership with your child's coach, teachers, and other adult mentors so you are on the same page regarding your child's development. Know your role.
3. Keep a proper balance between sports, school, spiritual growth, and family.
4. Recognize the achievements of all your kids and not just your athletes.
5. Block time for all your kids and not just your athletes.
6. Block time for yourself, make sure you exercise and eat well, and model perspective for your children.
7. Live so that your children know they are the most important thing in your life, but they are not the only important thing.
8. We don't get any do-overs, so live your life as if this is all there is.

Game-Changing Question for Parents

Take a look at the following statement and decide whether you strongly agree, agree, disagree, or strongly disagree with it:

When it comes to my children's sports, I keep everything in perspective.

If you don't like your answer, ask yourself "What am I going to do about it?"

Be Patient

One of the crucial components of taking a common-sense approach to sports is to practice patience. It is imperative to recognize how hard it is to learn a sport. It is as hard as learning math or reading or history. It takes time, and you need to have the patience to let your child learn a sport, just as you do in school. We don't have them take their year-end exams in September, so common sense tells us we shouldn't do it with sports either. This is often easier said than done, as we get front-row seats every Saturday to their "sporting tests." Just take a deep breath, remember that this is a journey, and enjoy the ride. This requires patience.

Think Math

As psychologist Dr. Dan Saferstein succinctly states in his booklet "Win or Lose: A Guide to Sports Parenting," think math! Imagine your son or daughter doing their math homework at your kitchen table every night. Do you stand behind them, moaning and groaning every time they forget to carry the one or put the decimal in the wrong place? Would you go to their math test on Friday and stand along the wall, oohing and ahhing at their every success or mistake? Of course not, because if this happened your kids could not complete their homework or show their competency on a test. They would feel too much pressure with the weight of your stare and your disapproval of their mistakes. Eventually they would say, "I hate math. I don't want to do it anymore because I am no good at it."

When my wife and I placed our kids in a Spanish Language Immersion kindergarten program in our hometown of Bend, Oregon, the director did not say that our kids would be fluent in two weeks. If she did we would have laughed and said "Thanks but no thanks, what a farce." What she did tell us was that by fifth grade, a full six years out, our kids would read, write, and speak Spanish and English at or above grade level. Six years! It was up to us to trust them, release them to the teachers, support them from home, and let our kids learn. But it made perfect sense, so we said yes.

So why is it that every Saturday parents of all shapes and sizes cheer, boo, yell, scream, and subject their kids to excessive micromanagement in their athletic experience? I spent twenty years coaching soccer, and I could not imagine ever asking a parent to keep writing checks and give me six years to teach their child how to play. I could not imagine telling them that it would take years for their son to learn to properly kick a ball, dribble, pass, think on the fly—and do it at full speed under tremendous opposition pressure. Why? They would have laughed at me if I told them to spend tens of thousands of dollars in equipment, fees, and travel to watch their son for the next six years, to be patient and wait for physical and mental maturity, as well as the educational process, to see itself out. Most likely they would have gone and given their money to someone who showed a little bang for the buck on a weekly basis.

The alarming dropout rate in organized sports in the United States has coincided with the growth of the "X Games" culture of sports such as skiing, snowboarding, skateboarding, biking, and others. These are all incredible sports, and they all have one thing in common. They are so new that most parents have not participated in them, have no idea how to do them, and thus when their kids take them up, these parents pretty much stay out of the way. They let the kids have fun and learn the sports at their own pace. Since their parents have no idea what the learning curve is, or how to do most of the required skills, kids set the educational timetable with no sense of urgency or parental anxiety. Parents do not compare their own athletic career with that of their kids, contrasting their experience in a sport that came easy to them with their kids who may be struggling and experiencing frustration as a result.

These sports force parents to demonstrate the very patience they struggled to provide during their child's traditional organized sports experience. There are very few parents out there who are capable of explaining the finer points of a "cork 720" to their son or daughter, for they have never even snowboarded, let alone tried such a trick. They usually just sit back and cheer for their child. They are often amazed and proud of their child's competency at something they are unable to do.

Put many of those same parents at a soccer game, though, and regardless of whether they have ever kicked a ball in their life, you'd think they had spent their entire lives learning the finer points of the game. "Clear it, Billy!" "Pass it, Suzie, she's wide open!" "Come on, Kevin, stop dribbling!" "Shoot it!" Is it any wonder why kids are flocking in droves to sports where they are not judged at every single game on every single play by nearly every parent on the team?

Trust Your Kids and Focus on the Right Results

I know many parents who are incredibly understanding of the learning process in some areas of life—often ones that they too struggled with—yet quite hard on their kids in areas that came easily to them. Most parents I know seem to be far more patient with things they are unfamiliar with than those areas they have competency in. Oftentimes parents are very understanding of academics, for most everyone had at least one subject that was a struggle. Yet why is it that we trust our kids to learn when it comes to academics, but when it comes to sports many of us feel an incessant need to correct every mistake? Why is trial and error okay for the student but unacceptable for the student athlete? I believe it comes down to one thing, and that is a lack of patience driven by an unrelenting focus on outcomes instead of the process.

An overemphasis on competition——as opposed to training——makes it easy to understand why many parents and coaches measure sports success in wins and losses. Our sports have become far more success oriented and far less developmentally focused. Yet these competitions are finite and short-lived. We measure results in time spans of two hours instead of two weeks, or two months instead of two years. The attitude is often "If I don't see improvement this weekend, we are finding you a new coach!"

A number of recent books, such as Dan Coyle's *The Talent Code* and Malcolm Gladwell's *Outliers*, demonstrate that true expertise comes from ten thousand hours of deliberate practice. This would not matter to many parents. I could show them how their daughter had visibly improved in her technique, her confidence, her athleticism, and her overall competence.

I could even show them how much their daughter loved to be with her friends and to come to training every day and improve. In most cases it would not make a difference, because far too many parents today do not look upon athletics the same way they do education, nor do they look at it as a part of their child's education.

Too many parents look at sports as a way to measure their child (and themselves) against other kids (and their parents). They give their kids sixty minutes on Saturday to learn to hit a curve ball or score a goal or make a save, and then moan and groan, hide their head in shame, and either directly or indirectly demonstrate to their kids their unhappiness at their failure.

Deep down we know that being patient with our kids is the only way they will ever learn trigonometry or reading, and that it is okay not to understand how to do things when you first begin learning them. As a result of our patience in the educational process, kids learn complicated mathematics, how to read and write, how to analyze and solve problems, and how to think critically. They do not fear the repercussions of every single mistake they make in the learning process. In many instances we have taken this away from them when it comes to sports.

What if the opposite were true? What would happen if we showed this same kind of patience in developing our young athletes? Why can't we judge our coaches on seasons and years rather than weekends? Hopefully, most of us don't call our kids' teachers on Friday and scream at them because our kids are confused after a week of physics, but I have seen parents lined up after a game waiting to explain to the coach what went wrong during the match, why Sally can't pass and Johnny can't kick, and demanding to know what the coach is going to do about it.

Kids' Games versus Adult Sports

There is a funny thing about youth sports that makes parents forget education is a process. When our kid's uniform goes on, some part of our brain switches off and we stop seeing kids running around on the field.

We start seeing mini-adults and place adult expectations upon them. I am not exactly sure why this happens, but my guess is that sports are usually the first activities kids do that resemble adult activities. The basic concepts of sports (i.e., kicking, throwing, running, catching) come somewhat naturally to adults, so we expect that they will come naturally to our kids. We forget that they come "naturally" because we have done them thousands of times before. Our kids have not, and thus the problem arises.

When our kids want to do a puzzle for the first time, we don't hand them the thousand-piece flower scene; we give them the ten-piece dinosaur puzzle. When our kids are learning to read, we don't hand them *War and Peace,* we give them *Dick and Jane.* And when we have our first catch, we don't toss a major league curve ball at them. This is common sense because all of us know that kids need to educate themselves on the fundamentals before they can advance to more difficult tasks, concepts, and movements. We display patience and realistic expectations, and we congratulate them for successfully completing tasks that are incredibly simple to us.

Now change gears for a second. Go to any youth soccer game this weekend and listen to what many of the parents are screaming at the players: "Kick it to Johnny," "Maddie is open; pick your head up and pass it to her," "Pace yourself out there, Tommy," "Don't kick it in the middle, Katie!" Because it is sports, and because our only experiences and memories with sports are adult ones, we instruct our kids in adult concepts. We cringe when they don't get it right away, and at worst we feel shame and embarrassment for their errors.

We forget that our children are in the process of learning. They do not need our help to prevent failure; they need us to help them overcome the fear of failure. Many beginning soccer players have no idea what goal they are trying to score in, where the boundaries of the field are, and at times what they are even doing out there. They don't pass it to teammates, they sometimes just dribble it too far and it goes to someone. They don't see the sideline or their teammates; they see a ball and some grass and a bunch of feet trying to kick their toy (the ball) away. They run as hard as they can for as long as they can, then they stop or sit down or just walk off for a drink. In fact, my favorite part about coaching U6 soccer is that players are just as excited when they score in their own goal as when they score in the opponents' goal! They have twice the opportunity to find success! It is beautiful.

Next time you are at your child's game, give the kids a break and understand that what they see and what you see are two completely different things. Forget everything you know about the game and try to imagine what their game looks like. Save your breath for some cheering and a post-game hug. Just let them play.

If you find yourself applying adult expectations to kids' games, try to refocus on the process of athletic development instead of weekly or monthly outcomes. Try to recognize that judging our kids on a single play, on a single game, or on a single season is incredibly shortsighted. We should step back and see the big picture and understand that the most important things our players will earn from athletics are learned over a lifetime, and that those kids who play the longest——and not necessarily play the best—get the most out of it. We need lifelong athletes who cannot wait to step on the field or get into the pool, who look forward to testing themselves, and who are able to fail again and again without repercussions or recriminations. We need patience! The questions below will help you assess your patience in your child's athletic education, and the Action Steps list some ways to help yourself be a patient parent.

Game-Changing Questions for Parents

Please complete the following sentences to assess your patience as a sports parent:

1. The reason my son/daughter plays sports is so that he/she will learn ...

2. For each of the reasons for playing above, fill in the blanks: When I was growing up, it took me approximately _____ to learn _____.
3. With these goals in mind, when I attend my son/daughter's competition, I encourage these goals by ...
4. With these goals in mind, when I attend my son/daughter's competition, I may be discouraging these goals by ...

Action Steps for Practicing Patience

1. Set process goals for a season, a year, and a lifetime instead of week by week.
2. Set achievable and actionable steps to reaching those goals so that you can chart progress, but recognize that each step is part of the journey and not the destination.
3. Keep these goals in mind when you attend games and practice, and educate your child with these goals in mind.

Be Grateful, Express Your Gratitude, and Teach Your Child to Do the Same

If we magnified blessings as much as we magnify disappointments, we would all be much happier.

—**John Wooden**, UCLA basketball coach

One of the best ways to keep a *common-sense* approach to youth sports is to be grateful. Express your gratitude each and every day for all the positive things in your life and the opportunities that your child has. Start by being grateful and you will be pleasantly surprised at how quickly and positively your outlook on things can change.

When I began writing this book, I realized that gratitude was missing from so many people's recollections of youth sports. I realized how many people chose to complain or gripe about the four things that were wrong in their life, on their team, or with their coach instead of focusing on the ninety-six things that were great. I started to ask my friends in coaching whether they noticed this as well. "Oh my God, yes!" was the nearly unanimous reply. "No one says thanks anymore."

When we really think about it, there are so many things that we should be grateful for. Start by being grateful that your child is healthy, happy, and has the opportunity to play sports. There are many countries around the world where your kids could not attend school or participate in athletics without fear of being shot or caught in some other random act of violence. There are many places where your daughter would not even be allowed to show herself in public or attend school, much less participate in sports.

Be grateful that you have the financial means to afford your child's participation in sports and other activities, or that your club has a scholarship fund that allows him to participate. Be thankful that you can afford the equipment, the travel, and the other necessary components of playing sports, instruments, or whatever activities your child does.

Be grateful for the coaches, the teachers, the volunteers, and the mentors in your child's life. Even if they are paid, they still do it out of love for sport, for service, and because they love helping kids. Express your gratitude to them, not just at season's end, but after a tough loss, or a difficult stretch or situation, or after they give your child some extra attention. Coaching and teaching can often be thankless, and most coaches I know stick with it for the kids and certainly not the money. An unexpected thanks at an unexpected time helps to fill coaches' emotional tanks and keep them going through the tough times.

As a coach and club director, I probably read ten times as many emails regarding problems and complaints as I did messages of thanks. I was told on more than one occasion when I suggested to a parent that he might thank his child's coach, "Why should I say thanks? That's what he is paid to do." Really? Is the extra time and caring that a coach or teacher shows your child not worth anything to you because they receive a small stipend?

I am confident that at your job you feel pretty good when your coworkers, clients, and superiors recognize you for your effort. I know it hurts when they ignore all your hard work and never say thank you. Why? Because most people are far more motivated by expressions of gratitude than by financial rewards. So why not do the same for the people in your child's life who give their time and knowledge to help you raise your child? It makes them feel good as well. And it works in your child's favor!

Here is a little hint. Coaches all love to say that they do not play favorites. But guess what? They do! And who are coaches' favorites? The kids who practice the hardest, give the best effort, pay attention, show improvement, and perhaps most importantly say THANK YOU! Give me two players of similar ability who display all of the above, and the kid I will start ten times out of ten is the one who says "Thanks, coach" after every practice, or the child of a parent who goes out of his way to say thanks. It's just human nature to show appreciation to those who appreciate you, so learn to say thanks, teach your child to express gratitude, and watch it come back to you tenfold.

When you express your gratitude, you also teach your kids to do the same. I remember my father teaching my siblings and me to always say thank you to our coaches as we were growing up. I never realized why until I became a coach and saw how few kids actually do that anymore. Season ending gifts are a nice gesture of thanks, but I would much rather have a team of kids who shook my hand after every practice and said "Thanks, coach, that was fun." That tells a coach the players appreciate the time and effort he or she has just put in on their behalf. It tells a coach that the players got something out of that session, and they appreciate it. A simple thanks means a lot.

If it makes you feel any better, I am not just talking the talk here. While I wrote this book I realized that I was not truly grateful enough for all the great things in my life. I realized I needed to make a change and show my kids what it means to express gratitude.

Since this realization, I have tried to wake up every morning and be thankful for all the amazing things in my life, for my amazing wife and beautiful kids. I have tried to be more grateful for the wonderful place I live, the friends I have, and the opportunities to work with so many awesome families and kids. I do the same when I go to sleep at night. During the day I try to say thanks to everyone who does something for me, no matter how small. I have also asked my kids to do the same. And when we sit down for dinner every night, everyone in our family is asked to say at least one thing they are grateful for that day before we eat.

I believe we are responsible for our own happiness in all aspects of our lives. It is easy to blame our misery on coaches, teammates, and situations beyond our control, but deep down I think we all realize that only we make ourselves unhappy, and only we can change that. Expressing your gratitude is a great way to focus on reasons for being happy and changing your entire demeanor and attitude toward sports and life.

Game-Changing Question for Parents

Am I properly expressing my gratitude and teaching my children to do the same?

Action Steps for Expressing Gratitude

1. Make an effort to say thank you to your friends, family, and coworkers each and every day.
2. Say thanks, and teach your child to say thanks, to his coaches, teachers, and other adult mentors.

3. Find things every day to be grateful for, and ask your family to do the same. Express your gratitude to each other and with each other.
4. Practice random acts of kindness (I know this is a bumper sticker, but it is a good one).
5. Keep a journal to inventory all the things in your life that you are grateful for.

Matching Your Actions to Your Intentions

As a parent of a young athlete, you might ask yourself a question such as this:

"Do my actions reflect the values I want my child to embody?"

I think this simple question helps you keep everything in perspective and ensures that every aspect of your child's athletic experience is leading toward the core values and life lessons you want them to garner from their sports experience. Unfortunately, many parents and coaches never ask themselves this simple question. They should because it is the basis of everything we are speaking about here.

Write this question down, or create your own version, but carry it with you always. When you choose a sports club or school for your child, ask yourself this question. When you find a coach for your child, ask this question. When you speak to your child, when you set goals with your child, when you praise or teach him, ask this simple question. Whenever you are in doubt or unsure about a situation, take a step back and ask "Do my actions reflect my values?"

If they do, chances are your child is headed toward a positive sports experience. If they don't, take heart that it is never too late to change how you act. Your kid today is a culmination of your past actions and words, and your future child will be built upon everything you do from this day forward.

Action Steps for Matching Your Actions with Your Intentions

1. Define your core values and the moral imperatives you want to pass onto your children.
2. Ask yourself whether the things you are doing today are modeling those goals.
3. Make changes if needed.

Game-Changing Questions for Your Child

1. The reasons I play sports are ...
2. The coaches and parents make sports enjoyable by ...
3. The coaches and parents make sports less enjoyable by ...

Game-Changing Activity for Your Family

Please take your answers to these questions and, combined with your child's answers, come up with your "Family Youth Sports Mission Statement." If you wish, include things such as:

- Purpose of sports
- Core values that are important to your family
- The reasons your child plays
- The ways the adults help your child enjoy sports
- The things to avoid that make sports less enjoyable

6

Conditions

*Young players play with great deal of fairness and sportsmanship.
Once they learn how important the game is to the adults, they'll
learn how to cheat.*

—Dr. Ron Quinn, professor of sports ethics,
Xavier University

"**B**ut the team wins all its games—that's good, isn't it?" I heard that question a lot as a coach, and now Jimmy's dad was asking it. "His mom and I just don't think he is getting the recognition and exposure here that he will on that team. That is why we are switching clubs." Exposure? Recognition? What about development, fun, and camaraderie? Has your child been on a team where some parents are always looking for greener pastures? Did I mention that Jimmy was eleven years old?

So often we only look to wins and losses as an indicator of a safe and developmentally appropriate sports environment. As we talked about earlier, this is one of the great myths of youth sports. The wins and losses do matter, but not necessarily the way you think they do.

Proper conditions are essential to creating a high-performance state of mind and are a requirement of a positive sports experience. It is your responsibility as a parent or coach to ensure that this environment is safe and focused on proper long-term athletic development. You have four primary responsibilities when identifying and selecting a healthy sports environment for your child:

1. Understanding the factors influencing sports performance
2. Understanding the science of long-term athletic development (LTAD)
3. Identifying, selecting, and ensuring a physically, mentally, and emotionally safe place to play
4. Helping your child learn and apply life lessons

I have found that many well-intentioned parents have no idea what it takes to become a high-performing athlete. It is not just talent or practice or coaching, but a combination of numerous factors. Nor do many parents—or coaches for that matter—understand and adhere to the latest findings about proper LTAD. These are crucial elements when it comes to selecting the coaches, clubs, and schools that will form your child's athletic education. These elements are often overlooked or undervalued compared to wins and losses, trophies and medals.

It is your parental responsibility to find a safe environment for your child. We live in a world where our children are often entrusted to adults we know very little about, and where a few of these adults commit unspeakable acts. As a parent, you should ensure that your child is safe, but not just physically. Their mental and emotional development is at stake here as well. Yet again, we often only look at wins and losses when it comes to choosing a coach or a club. We need to look at how those wins and losses were achieved and whether the coach, school, or club is teaching the core values and life lessons you just listed for yourself.

Your responsibility does not begin and end when you drop your child at practice or game. Your actions at home play a large role in determining whether your child feels safe in sports. Are you allowing your child to fail and learn from their mistakes, or are you solving everything for them and micromanaging their athletic education? Do your kids feel that your love is tied to athletic success, or are you supporting them emotionally and encouraging them to have fun, learn new things, and go out and experience all this world has to offer? Use these questions to assess your young athlete's environment, as they are critical to developing happy and high-performing athletes.

The Factors Determining Athletic Performance

Don't measure yourself by what you have accomplished, but by what you should have accomplished with your ability.
—**John Wooden**, UCLA basketball coach

Athletic performance is determined by a number of factors. As we spoke about earlier, results come from the interplay of intentions, state, and actions. I believe it all boils down to the following equation:

Talent + State of Mind + Coaching + Deliberate Practice + Luck = Performance

Maximum performance depends upon all of these components. Not enough talent, no motivation, poor coaching, and unfocused practice all lead to diminished performance, just as exceptional genes, a trigger event, great coaching, and hours of training can yield an elite performer. In our world of incessant need for control, I hate to say it but a little good luck goes a long way, just as some bad luck or an injury might lead to diminished performance. There are many factors at work here.

Talent

Whether we like to admit it or not, genes play a part in our performance potential. You can have an incredibly motivated and well-coached athlete, but without good genes he may never play in the NBA or run in the Olympics. Sure, things like strength, speed, and agility can be trained to a point, but ultimately some of us are built to excel at certain athletic activities that may require fast-twitch muscle capabilities, while others of us might do better with slow-twitch activities such as endurance running or cycling. We are not all sprinters, nor are we all distance runners.

Conversely, an athlete with incredible genes but no work ethic or motivation will not achieve his or her potential. It takes thousands of hours of training and extreme motivation to achieve elite performing status.

Ultimately, becoming an elite athlete is not the be-all and end-all goal of sports. There are plenty of reasons to participate in sports and plenty of things to be learned from athletics that have nothing to do with elite performance. Yet in the end, in terms of general, overall performance, genes do play a part.[13]

State of Mind

Motivated and passionate athletes who devote the most time and energy to a sport, and enjoy themselves while participating, are often the highest achievers. High performers need a growth-oriented mindset and support of growth-mindset adults.

While it is difficult and potentially detrimental for a parent to constantly motivate a young athlete, you can give him the tools and create the environment for him to be self-motivated. These are the 7 Cs. Kids need some control over the process, a degree of competency, conditions that nurture confidence, and unconditional love. You can let the game belong to them, you can provide perspective and balance, and from time to time you can give a slight push in the right direction. When you help your child take on the right state of mind, the passion and dedication will eventually come from him.

Children also need ignition, something that piques their interest in a sport. It may be as simple as stopping to watch the local pick-up basketball game at your neighborhood park and taking note of your child's interest. Or it may be an international event, such as the effect of the 1999 Women's World Cup victory by the USA on girls' youth soccer, or Tiger Woods's popularity in growing the game of golf. A local athlete may make the major leagues or qualify for the Olympics, and it will spark interest in a sport in your area.

Look for these signs and nurture them. If your child is asking questions about the famous women's soccer stars Mia Hamm or Abby Wambach, take her home and watch some videos on You Tube. Ask her if she would like to try soccer, and sign her up for a local league. Go out in the backyard and kick a ball around with her. Take her to a college or high school game. Whatever you do, take note of the spark, and fan the flames of interest.

Coaching

Great coaching can play a huge role in athletic performance and take many forms. A great coach may take the form of a master coach who has developed world-class athletes and knows the finer points of technique, tactics, and motivation. Or she might be a local mom who just knows how to make kids fall in love with soccer or running or tennis. In fact, I have found that it is more important for coaches of young kids to understand children, as opposed to having a deep knowledge of a sport.

The best coaches have a growth mindset and know how to motivate, communicate, and inspire their athletes to achieve more than they ever would on their own. They instill a love of the game, a passion for achievement, and model the character and values that they preach to their athletes. They know when a kid needs a hug and when he needs a metaphoric kick in the rear. All high performers can point to various coaches as major contributors in their ultimate success, and most lifelong athletes can point to a coach who taught them to love sport and to be active for life.

Deliberate Practice

The subject of deliberate practice, the ten-thousand-hour rule, has gotten a lot of coverage recently, due to books such as Dan Coyle's *The Talent Code*, Malcolm Gladwell's *Outliers*, and Matthew Syed's *Bounce*. The premise is that elite performance, whether in athletics, music, or computer programming, comes after approximately ten thousand hours of focused training. While there is some debate over whether these authors have placed too much emphasis on practice at the expense of a multitude of other factors that affect performance, there is no question that the amount of time one spends practicing plays a huge role in skill development.

Deliberate practice is dedicated, focused training on a particular subject or activity. By repeating the techniques and skills required to perform said activity, we promote the development of myelin, a fatty tissue that insulates our nervous system. Like any wire, the more insulation a nerve has, the faster it can transmit signals. By myelinating our skill-specific nerves through repetitive activity, we become more proficient and thus better performers.

The concept that ten thousand hours is required to become an elite performer—to properly myelinate our nerves—was put forth by Anders Ericcson in a 1993 study on violin players. He found that the best experts had accumulated ten thousand hours of study by the age of twenty, while less accomplished violinists had accrued a smaller amount of training. This study, and others like it, has been highlighted by the authors mentioned above to give credence to their theory that ten thousand hours of deliberate practice is the reason for success. However, ten thousand hours of training is not the be-all and end-all of elite performance, as recent work has shown that some elite performers have achieved world-class status with only a few thousand hours of training. That said, hard work and dedicated training are certainly a huge factor and determinant of athletic performance.[14]

Luck

Finally, all elite performers can point to a piece of luck somewhere along the line that allowed them to stake their claim and rise to the top. John Daly won the PGA after getting in as a last-second alternate. A young baseball player named Lou Gehrig got his shot to break into the Yankees when star first baseman Wally Pipp decided to take a day off. Luck plays a role. I think we might agree that while no high achiever is such solely because of luck, most elite performers can point to a bit of luck along the path to success.

Performance

The culmination of talent, motivation, coaching, practice, and luck determines the level of performance of an athlete. Placing them in a safe and developmentally appropriate environment plays a large role in this. And the best science regarding long-term athletic development comes from our neighbors to the north, Canada.

Long-Term Athletic Development (LTAD)

Canadian Sport For Life (CS4L) was founded in 2005 to provide sport developmental guidelines for coaches, parents, educators, and others involved in Canadian youth sports. CS4L found major issues affecting Canadian sports, among them:

- The youngest Canadian athletes were not learning proper movement and fundamental athletic skills and therefore never achieved proper skill development, fitness, and optimal performance as they grew older.

- Inexperienced coaches were providing the vast majority of instruction at the most crucial ages for development.
- The overemphasis on competition led to the formation of bad habits.
- The under-emphasis on training prevented athletes from breaking bad habits and forming good ones.
- With no streamlined developmental system in place, athletes were pulled in multiple directions by clubs, schools, select and national teams, with each organization placing them on different developmental paths.
- These conflicting environments were taking the fun out of sports, inhibiting proper development, and leading to poor performance, or worse, young people giving up athletics.
- Parents were not educated in developmental principles and therefore did not know what to look for in their child's athletic programs.
- Sports were specializing too early in an attempt to attract and retain participants.

Sound familiar?

The primary goal of CS4L is to overcome the above issues facing young Canadian athletes and combat the rise in obesity and overall poor health. To accomplish their goals, CS4L has developed the long-term athletic development model.

LTAD refers to the framework of athlete education and development that can be used to teach our parents, coaches, and administrators about optimal ways to educate and develop high-performing athletes. LTAD focuses on developmental rather than chronological age and links athlete education with their physical and psychological growth, as opposed to calendar years. Developed in part by internationally recognized coaching educator Istvan Balyi, the LTAD model aggregates widely accepted principles of athletic development that have been the basis of physical education for years. As of the writing of this book, over one hundred major national and international sporting federations have adopted the principles of LTAD as the basis for new player and coaching education programs.[15]

Physical Literacy

The main goal of the CS4L program is to develop physical literacy in young athletes (twelve and under). Physical literacy is defined as acquiring the fundamental movement skills and sports skills that need to be *learned* as a child, so that children will feel good about participation in physical activities. Note that there is emphasis on learned, as not all children have these skills innately, nor do they come as easily for some as they do for others. They must be taught.

This is an important point and should not be overlooked. Think of it this way: what would you do if your first grader was struggling with reading? You would get extra help, spend more time, and teach him how to read, for you know that reading is an essential life skill. When it comes to kids and sports, though, many parents say "my kid is not athletic" and allow him to quit before he even gets started. I would argue that physical literacy is as essential as reading if one wants to live a fulfilling and balanced life. We need to teach those kids who do not pick up sports easily; we should not be writing off six-year-olds as "un-athletic" and "no good at sports."

I once had a conversation with a mom about this, as she had five-year-old twin boys. One, she told me, loved all sports and was a great athlete. The other, well, he was just not much of an athlete so he did not do any athletic activities. She had decided that her son, at five years old, would never be an athlete because he did not take to sports like his brother. Since they did not come naturally, he did not like sports. No one had ever told her it was her job to teach these fundamental movement skills. I urged her to enroll her son again and to teach him just as she would teach him to read. He needed to learn his ABCs!

Physical literacy involves learning the ABCs of agility, balance, coordination, and speed so that children possess the ability to move confidently and appropriately on the field or in the arena of their chosen sport or activity. The goal is to increase ability in all types of athletic activity, for the science shows that when children become more competent, they participate more vigorously, play for longer durations, and perform better.

As a parent of a young child, it is imperative that you put them in an environment that teaches the movements and skills of physical literacy. This does not mean only organized sports programs. This can be backyard play, running and jumping at the playground, swimming or sledding with the family, or riding your bikes. In the first three stages of LTAD (ages 0-12), parents are at the forefront in promoting physical literacy. Some kids figure these movements and skills out on their own. Others do not and must be taught and encouraged to learn.

Seven Stages of LTAD

CS4L has broken up long-term athletic development into seven stages based upon the newest science, research, and on-the-ground experience in athletics, coaching, and education. Their methodology demonstrates that by introducing and training the correct skills at the right times of development, both kids and adults will become more active, stay active, and perform better than those who do not follow such a program. The seven stages are:

1. Active Start (ages 0-6)
2. FUNdamentals (girls 6-8, boys 6-9)
3. Learn to Train (girls 8-11, boys 9-12)
4. Train to Train (girls 11-15, boys 12-16)
5. Train to Compete (girls 15-21, boys 16-23)

6. Train to Win (girls 18+, boys 19+)
7. Active for Life (any age)

The first three stages are designed to teach children physical literacy. These stages teach movement and sport fundamentals before children reach puberty so that they have the basic skills needed to remain active for life. They also provide a foundation for elite-level competition at the older ages if that is the path the child chooses.

Stages 4-6 are for the elite training of athletes. They are for children who choose to focus on a specific sport or sports and are designed to maximize the physical, mental, and emotional development of each athlete. Stage 7 is focused on taking these properly developed athletes and making them lifelong participants in recreational and competitive sports, as well as promoting an active lifestyle. Let's explore each stage in more depth and then discuss what the unfortunate reality is in terms of development in youth sports in Canada, the United States, and beyond.

Stage 1: Active Start: Children ages 0-6 need to engage in daily, unstructured active play by themselves and with their peers to develop the foundational movements needed to become active for life. Not only will they develop physical coordination and motor skills, but an early active start enhances development of brain function, posture, and balance. It also helps children to become confident, gain emotional control, and develop both social skills and imagination while at the same time reducing stress and improving sleep. A wide variety of physical activities should be introduced. Most importantly, the activities in this phase should be seen by children as fun and engaging parts of a day.

The brain develops rapidly the first three years of life, forming pathways and connections much faster than in later years. As a result, an active start to development improves coordination and balance as well as helps kids learn more efficiently and confidently. It improves emotional development, imagination, and leadership while building strong muscle and bone and promoting a healthy weight and lifestyle.

It is critical at this stage that parents make sure activity is a fun, safe, and voluntary undertaking; kids should not be "required" to partake. It is also a great stage for parents to join their kids, to run, jump, and laugh alongside them and model the skills and techniques for kids to learn. Kids learn by doing and by modeling what others do, so jump right in. The basic foundational movements of crawling, walking, running, and jumping come naturally to kids as their bodies develop the proper strength and coordination skills to perform them. Kids develop these basic skills when they are encouraged to do so, surrounded by active children and adults to model and provided a safe environment in which to experiment. Don't forget to let them take charge once in a while—they might surprise you. Be a participant in your child's active start, and who knows, you both may benefit!

Stage 2: FUNdamentals: During the FUNdamental stage, girls ages 6-8 and boys ages 6-9 should be exposed to a wide variety of athletic experiences. Kids should be changing activities season to season to avoid burnout and boredom. These activities can be structured but should still focus on FUN; competitive games and matches should be kept to a minimum. Kids begin to read the game going on around them and thus can make decisions, and movements, about what is happening during the match. Let them see the game, and try not to see it for them!

The FUNdamental stage is one of the sensitive times to develop hand and foot speed through fun activities and games, and not training regimens and drills. Every sport can develop these skills, and even a soccer coach can be working on catching while jumping, running, even doing forward rolls. If your child has a preferred sport, there is nothing wrong with him participating two to three times a week, but make sure he is doing other sports or activities three times a week as well. This well-rounded approach helps to master all aspects of physical literacy and keeps the child excited and engaged.

While your child might be involved in some sports that keep score at this stage, remember that his focus will not be on the score, but more on being with friends and having fun. Make sure your focus is there as well. Help them to focus on fun and develop self-confidence and belief in their ability, and you have already won regardless of any score that is kept.

Stage 3: Learn to Train: Girls (8-11) and boys (9-12) begin to convert their foundational movements into basic sports skills during this stage, which CS4L calls the "Golden Age of Learning" for sports. If you think about it, this makes perfect sense as this stage comes to a close when the child hits puberty, the growth spurt occurs, and there is a temporary loss of coordination and motor control. This is the best time to learn sport-specific skills as the child is still in control of his body and can see daily and weekly improvement from his hard work. This is the sensitive period of accelerated skill development and must not be overlooked or shortchanged by overemphasizing competition (as often happens).

Unless your child is doing an early specialization sport, such as gymnastics or skating, they should still participate in a wide variety of sports during this stage. That said, they can begin to focus on developing sport-specific skills during those training hours. The emphasis should continue to be on more training and less competition, with at least a 2:1 or 3:1 ratio of practice to games. This is a great time to develop strength, flexibility, and some stamina, but through relays, fun activities, and training without supplemental weights instead of physically demanding regimens.

One very interesting thing to note about the Learn to Train stage is that it can be either a great advantage to a late-developing athlete or a great disadvantage. With excellent coaching, in a proper development environment, a young athlete who hits puberty later than her classmates has a longer period in which to develop fundamental and sport specific skills. She remains in the "Golden Age" longer than her peers, and if she takes advantage of this extra time, her technical skill base can surpass the early developers.

Unfortunately, oftentimes late developers are overlooked for select-level sports teams simply because they have not grown, they are not as strong, and they are not as fast. The overemphasis on competition at these young ages funnels out these late developers as coaches pick the biggest and strongest players for success in competition. This is a worrying trend, for studies show that over the long term the late developers who are kept within the high-level training regimen become better long-term performers because of a better skill base.

If your child is in this stage, and she is a late developer, make sure she is in the right coaching and developmental environment. She should continue to focus on her skills and not things like strength and speed, which will come naturally a bit later. Many times as a soccer club director I saw parents trying to get their late-developing son to lift weights and get stronger so they could play against the big guys, when the focus should have been on doubling down on the skill development. Five years down the road, the kids with the extra skill are now the same size, the same speed, and are usually the better players.

Stage 4: Train to Train: The Train to Train stage (girls 11-15, boys 12-16) is the first of three stages in the high-performance training and competition development stream. It is a time for enhancement of sport-specific skills, building an aerobic base, and overall development of long-term athletic potential. As you can see by the age range, this stage begins at the onset of puberty and ends at the conclusion of the adolescent growth spurt. Train to Train is where athletes become more sport-specific and ramp up their training hours as they begin to specialize in a chosen sport and usually compete in a second, complementary sport. In the end, the development done here makes Train to Train the make-or-break stage for becoming an elite performer in a specific sport.

It is crucial to remember that winning should remain secondary to skill and physical development, although competition can be ramped up at this time as athletes test their skills against fellow competitors. Every sport has different requirements at this stage, but the emphasis is still on development, education, and progression. It is not measured by wins and losses.

It is incredibly important during this stage to recognize, and explain to athletes, that their coordination and movement may be affected by their growth spurt and that this is perfectly normal. Coaches and parents must assure kids that the negative effect on their physical abilities is natural and will pass. It is also crucial to work on flexibility, and at the correct times strength. Training to competition ratio should be 60:40, and again, the competition should be used to enhance tactical understanding and physical ability, not to measure outcomes. In fact, CS4L has found that *the reason many athletes plateau later in their development is because during this stage they shifted their focus from training to competition and did not complete their skill development.*

Stage 5: Train to Compete: Train to Compete (girls 15-21, boys 16-23) is the stage where athletes choose a specific sport to become an elite competitor in, focusing on high-volume and high-repetition training. This is a stage that elite competitors enter, and not your everyday recreational athletes. These players have aspirations of high school, collegiate, professional, and perhaps national and international competition in mind. Besides their sport-specific training, they also need to receive the instruction in nutrition, psychology, recovery, and injury prevention/management. Competition is at a premium, and athletes must set up proper periodization schedules, competition and recovery plans, and focus on consistent high-level performances.

Elite performers in the Train to Compete stage are not only maximizing their physical, mental, and psychological abilities, but they are also learning how to deal with external elements such as travel, media, spectators, and difficult opponents. They are selecting specific competitions and tailoring their training regimens to achieve maximum performance at these events. They are overemphasizing training at certain times, tapering for events, and allowing adequate rest and recovery after events. This is high-level training, heavy-duty commitment, and not the typical sporting experience for the vast majority of athletes.

Stage 6: Train to Win: Train to Win athletes are full-time competitors, seeking to win national and international events, playing professionally or at the highest level their sport allows, and dedicating themselves to the pursuit of not only excellence but success in terms of trophies, medals, and podiums. Athletes in this stage generally are 18+ for women's sports and 19+ for men. The skill training, tactical education, and physical growth are complete, or close to it, and now it is all about results. The full-time focus of this stage is on competition and results. If your athlete is at this stage an elite professional-level performer in his sport, congratulations. I am sure he has a support network of coaches, physicians, nutritionists, and yes, great parents working with him on a daily basis or he would not be there. Since this book is focused upon the other 99 percent of athletes, I will leave it at that, except to say congratulations to you and your child for advancing this far. It is an amazing accomplishment.

Stage 7: Active for Life: This is not only a stage but a primary goal of long-term athletic development—the creation of lifelong athletes who are healthier, happier, and active from childhood through adulthood. Active for life is a philosophy which stresses that lifelong participation in sports and other activities is not just for elite athletes but for all adults if we want to promote better health and wellness throughout our country and the world. It is not age- or gender-specific, and athletes can enter it at any time in life.

Being active for life does not only refer to on-the-field activities. It is also a call upon former athletes to give back by being coaches, mentors, administrators, officials, and policy makers in sport. It calls for athletes to "pay it forward" if you will, teaching the developmental philosophies and life lessons they learned to the next generation, while modeling and maintaining an active lifestyle.

In a way, Active for Life is also the goal of this book, as we are all responsible to ensure that our kids become lifelong athletes. Being active for life starts at the beginning. It is the end result of developing physical literacy in the younger years, which breeds a comfort with sports and a self-confidence about one's ability to participate. Early development of physical literacy becomes the foundation of a healthy adult, one who adheres to the principles of sound nutrition and exercise and models that same behavior for their children. This is one of the greatest gifts we can give our kids: the love of sports and the desire to be active throughout life!

Game-Changing Question for Parents

Are my children's sports and activities providing a level of training and games consistent with proper LTAD principles? If not, what am I going to do about it?

The Implementation of LTAD

In Canada, Australia, and Great Britain, national sport federations have adopted the LTAD principles into their sport-specific curriculums and are changing the way sports are run at the highest levels. This central approach is already yielding results, as evidenced by British advances in cycling and Australian advances in international swimming and basketball. The LTAD model has become the new sporting model for countries looking to both develop elite-level athletes and improve the overall health of their population.

In the United States, we have no central sports authority that governs all sports, and thus we depend upon a loose conglomeration of federations, associations, and governing bodies that vary from sport to sport, even state to state. This has worked for us for decades, due to our wealth and large population. American youth sports entities have thus clung to the status quo. As a result, other countries with far smaller populations are catching up in sports ranging from track to golf to basketball. While we continue to depend upon mass participation numbers that eventually lead to the emergence of elite athletes across a variety of sports, other countries are doing much more with much less. Uruguay and Portugal, with populations similar to my home state of

Oregon, are among the top-five soccer countries in the world right now. Why? A variety of factors to be sure, but none is more important than proper long-term athletic development.

Thankfully, a few governing bodies in American sports are beginning to encourage the LTAD model. Soccer, swimming, and hockey are a few of the sports that have recognized that the current system is broken. Unfortunately, the national federations have very little say over the actions of all the various entities that sponsor their sports. It seems this is starting to change. It will change even more as parents are educated about the importance of LTAD. Until then we can only hope that we have some "Sports Reaganomics" if you will, where LTAD philosophy trickles down into every community, every club, and every school.

Ten Key Factors of LTAD

CS4L has identified ten key factors of long-term athletic development, encompassing everything from the length of time it takes to achieve elite performance levels to the importance of program integration in terms of training and competition. The ten key factors are:

Ten-Year Rule: It takes ten thousand hours, or about ten years of deliberate practice (three hours a day), to achieve elite-level performance. This can include blended physical activity, and not necessarily sport-specific training, as early specialization can actually have a detrimental effect on performance.

FUNdamentals: The basic movement and sport skills children learn through fun activities that encourage a love of athletics and maintain their interest. These movements need to be learned prior to puberty and are designed to develop the ABCs of physical literacy: agility, balance, coordination, and speed.

Specialization: Identifying the right and wrong times, depending upon the specific sport, at which to specialize. Late-specialization athletes in sports such as soccer and hockey have more success if they participate in multiple sports in their preteen years, whereas in sports such as gymnastics and figure skating, elementary-age specialization results in increased performance.

Developmental Age: Every sport needs to take into consideration a child's stage of growth and development when designing training, games, and recovery activities. This does not just refer to chronological age but to the physical, mental, emotional, and intellectual maturity of the athlete (developmental age).

Trainability: Every athlete has certain periods where they are more receptive and sensitive to training in the areas of stamina, strength, speed, skill, and suppleness. It is up to coaches and parents to recognize when athletes are in these sensitive periods and take advantage of that period by maximizing training in that area.

Physical, Mental, Cognitive, and Emotional Development: LTAD is a holistic approach to development, and all training, competition, and recovery must take into account not only the physical component but the mental, emotional, and cognitive development of the athlete.

Periodization: Proper development breaks the athletes' training, competition, and recovery into cycles of participation. This starts with training sessions and moves to training weeks, to months, to seasons, and even to multiple-year cycles. The goal is to maximize performance at specific times while minimizing the chances of injury and burnout.

Competition Planning: Developing proper ratios of competition to training that *serves the needs of athletes, and not coaches, parents, and administrators.* Young athletes need to train far more than they compete, but unfortunately organized athletics in the United States and Canada has inverted this ratio and most kids play more than they train. This leads to injury and burnout. Proper ratios lead to better performance.

System Alignment and Integration: Proper LTAD requires schools, clubs, regional and national sporting organizations to collaborate and align their programs to achieve better development and performance from young athletes

Continuous Improvement: LTAD is a continually evolving and improving program, constantly integrating the latest in sport science, psychology, technology, and human performance.

These ten key factors form the foundational principles of long-term athletic development. Their adaptation by the various entities that control sport will eventually allow integrated systems to emerge that will produce higher performing and longer term athletes than our current uncoordinated and competing developmental systems. Most importantly, the end result will be an increase in the number of active adults and lifelong athletes, which will improve overall wellness and health.

Turning LTAD Theory into Practice

Hopefully this brief overview of long-term athletic development has given you a sense of where our coaches, administrators, and educators are headed with sports in the United States, Canada, and elsewhere. Are you thinking of your own children, the stages they are in, and whether their athletic programs are conforming with the best practices outlined by LTAD? Are you thinking that you may need to make a change in programs or add a few sports to make sure your child has the proper athletic education to become a lifelong athlete? I know when I first read this I thought long and hard about the activities my kids were participating in. Were they developing their physical literacy in their everyday play? Were they in a developmentally appropriate environment?

While the LTAD model looks great on paper, it is going to be a struggle to implement it. The current state of American youth athletics does not adhere to proper long-term development. The various competing entities in many sports are so busy fighting for participants (i.e., paying customers) that there is no integration of systems and a huge overemphasis on competition instead of training. In a nutshell, whoever offers the most games, the best games, and oftentimes the highest price tag usually gets the customers. Unfortunately, many organizations that are trying to do it right end up being the farm system for the clubs that emphasize winning at an early stage. It must change.

I for one hope the change will come from the top, from national governing bodies and state and local organizations, but I fear it will not. These organizations have the power to sanction the schools, the clubs, and the competitions that deal directly with the kids, and expel the members who do not follow proper LTAD models. Yet, due to the almighty dollar, all too often these organizations back away from their responsibility to lead for fear of losing customers and sponsors. The amount of money being made off youth athletics in the United States alone is staggering, and the corporate might behind many tournaments, championships, and national organizations does not necessarily have the same long-term goals as those organizations do.

I believe that true long-term athletic development will only come when our parents demand it from their clubs, their schools, their recreation departments, and all athletic service providers. It is up to us to ask why when these models are not being followed. We need to put our money where our mouth is by supporting organizations that adhere to proper LTAD. Our money talks in a big way, and we need it to start speaking up.

Providing a Safe Environment

Your greatest responsibility as a parent is that of finding and maintaining a safe athletic environment for your child. YOU are responsible for:

- Putting your child in a situation that is safe, both physically and emotionally
- Making sure that environment will teach life lessons and values to your child
- Making sure those life lessons are understood and applied on and off the field

There is no getting around being a responsible parent for your young athlete in this day and age. There are too many dangers lurking around every corner, with snake oil salesmen looking to sell you a bill of goods, guaranteed success, trophies, and college scholarships. It is up to you to be educated and to evaluate (and consistently reevaluate) the situation your child is in. Be aware of their goals, their ambitions, and their reasons for playing. Your child needs a parent with the life experience and perspective to place her in a good environment, to help her make good decisions, to learn the proper lessons sports should be teaching her, and at times to overrule her preferences if you believe an environment is unsafe or dangerous.

Identifying a Safe Environment for Your Child

We all know a parent whose kid is always on the winning side, who jumps from team to team and coach to coach, constantly positioning his ten-year-old for the guaranteed scholarship and the inevitable state championship. If you have been involved in youth sports long enough, you know who I am talking about and probably have a few names swirling in your head right now.

Parents often place their children in athletic environments that are unhealthy because of an incessant need to be a winning parent and to stroke their own ego. For many parents, teams, and organizations, winning takes precedence over educating and developing young athletes.

When it comes to athletics, for some families everything goes out the window in terms of finding a safe environment for kids. I have never seen a parent willingly put their child in a drivers' education car with an instructor who has had fifteen accidents, or in a classroom where all the students fail the state exam and are verbally abused by the teacher. Yet dangle the concept of a state championship or a college scholarship in front of a hungry parent and they willingly throw caution to the wind. They happily put their child in a sporting environment that teaches and tolerates values contrary to the principles they expect in every other aspect of their child's development and education.

I am not saying winning is a bad thing, or that I did not love to win games or championships as a coach. Winning should be a player's goal each and every time he steps on the field. Players must play to win or they are not giving 100 percent effort, which should be required of them every game. As a coach and as a parent, though, you must realize that winning in youth sports has nothing to do with the final score. It has everything to do with the end result, which is a happy, healthy child who performs his best and becomes an athlete for life.

True "winners" adhere to the guiding values and principles of their organization, and they strive to teach and emulate them day in and day out. Winning coaches demand a quest for excellence rather than short-term successes. But excellence requires patience, and many parents and coaches don't have the patience to achieve excellence. They see standings and game results as the only true measure of winning and thus put children in environments that stunt rather than enhance their growth.

As a coach or a parent of young athletes, it is your responsibility to make sure that development, and teaching life values, takes precedence over the final score. Evaluations should be conducted season by season and year by year, not game by game. In a match, effort and focus are what should be judged, never the scoreboard. Good coaches and parents model good behavior, they practice what they preach, and they always put developing excellence over winning a game. It is true that great coaches may win lots of games, but they never win by ignoring their values, principles, and core beliefs. They win because teaching excellence breeds success; they also realize that preaching success rarely yields excellence.

Physical Safety

It is critically important that your child's sports environment be a safe one. Environmental safety refers to:

Your child's overall health and conditioning: Make sure your child is cleared by your doctor to participate in sports, and after an injury, again cleared by a doctor to resume participation.

Proper nutrition and hydration: Most kids do not drink enough water or eat a diet conducive to athletic performance. Sports is a great way to improve your entire families' eating and drinking habits and to recognize what foods help performance and which ones hinder it.

Proper equipment: Out-of-date protective equipment can be extremely dangerous, and ill-fitting shoes can lead to blisters or far worse injuries. Make sure your child is properly equipped to play their sport of choice.

Injury prevention and treatment: From first aid kits to CPR training, there should be an adult on site who is capable of dealing with injuries as they occur. Most sports clubs also do injury prevention programs, such as limited pitch counts and knee injury prevention exercises.

Safety goes beyond your child's physical well-being and also refers to the environment he is placed in. No one should ever leave their child in the care of a coach, volunteer, or administrator they feel uncomfortable with. Despite the fact that nearly every sporting organization requires its coaches and volunteers to undergo background checks, every week around the country there are instances where known sexual predators have slipped through the cracks and are around children. If it can happen at Penn State University, it can happen at your local club.

Parents cannot turn a blind eye to the fact that danger may lurk around every corner for our kids, and we cannot bury our head in the sand. We have a responsibility to educate ourselves, and we cannot be indifferent, hoping nothing will happen to our child. There is no profile for sexual predators; they may be rich or poor, high IQ or low-functioning. They may be good-looking and well-mannered, and are often not the scruffy and disheveled characters we see in mug shots on TV. We must do our due diligence to ensure that whomever we entrust our children with are safe and responsible.

How important is this? The U.S. Department of Justice reports that 96 percent of all sexual assaults were perpetrated by males, and 23 percent of those were assaults by males under age eighteen. Over two-thirds of victims are under the age of eighteen, and more than half of those are under the age of twelve. More worrying is that over 90 percent of sexual assaults were committed by an acquaintance of the victim. For children under six, only 3 percent of assaults were committed by a stranger; that figure only rises to 5 percent for children ages six to eleven. The point here is not to lock your child in your home. It is to make sure that when you choose the athletic environment for your child, you are doing your research, considering all factors in your decision, and not basing it solely on wins and losses. If a child is one of the unfortunate few who are a victim of sexual abuse, it is likely to come from an acquaintance, not a stranger. As a parent, I find these statistics scary.

In their book *Education and Empowerment for the 21ˢᵗ Century Parent*, Dr. Albert Oppedisano and Dr. Aaron Cannon conclude:

> A very real and vital difference exists between healthy denial and purposeful indifference. As a parent, you need to make every possible effort to ensure the safety of your child (and then have trust and faith in those strategies) versus simply hoping that "nothing bad will happen to my child." Parents cannot blindly rely on other people's good nature. A thorough risk assessment includes getting as much history as possible on those individuals in charge of watching your children. Use the Internet, talk to other parents, and ask for references. You need to gather data from multiple sources to uncover useable information. You must first be as sure as you can reasonably be of others' intentions and good nature before you allow them to be responsible for your kids.[16]

Once you have satisfied yourself regarding the caregivers and coaches you are entrusting your child with, there are more physical safety elements to be concerned with. Safety also refers to the training and game environment created by your coach, your school, or your club. Are the training surfaces safe, is the training age and ability appropriate, are players given adequate rest and hydration? Long gone are the days of "run till you puke" and Bear Bryant's Junction Boys, whether you have fond memories of that kind of thing or not. I am all for mental toughness, but putting a child's life in danger by withholding hydration, or continuing extreme training in dangerous heat and humidity, is not the way to get the most out of our athletes.

I believe physical safety goes one step further. When a parent is researching a team or club you must make sure that dangerous play is not allowed or encouraged (if it is allowed, then it is indirectly being encouraged). Will a teenage player lose their head from time to time and commit a hard foul, dirty check, or bad tackle? Of course, as we all know that comes with being a teenager. But what happens next is what really matters the most.

Does the coach reprimand the player, discipline that player, and show remorse for the player's actions—or does the player leave the field with a high five from his coach, while his assistant coach screams at the officials? Does a certain team or school always lead the league in ejections, red cards, penalty minutes, etc.? If so, that is not a player issue, that is a coaching and values issue, and putting your child in that coaching environment is unsafe and dangerous, yet many parents do it. God forbid little Johnny forgets to put on his seatbelt; all hell breaks loose with mom and dad. But offer Johnny a spot on the state championship team with the loudmouth coach and the foulmouthed players who always win and Johnny's dad can't wait to cut that $3000 check. For if he doesn't, there are five more dads with backup offers!

Emotional Safety

You must look for an environment that is safe from an emotional standpoint as well. The coach that is constantly punishing players both mentally and physically should be a thing of the past, but it is not. It has been proven time and again that a 5:1 ratio of positive to negative comments provides children with the best education and motivation to be successful. The coach that is constantly pointing out the negative, and never providing praise when it has been earned, is dangerous for your child and will lead to their emotional breakdown.

It happens on all levels. In fact, one of my brother's worst sports memories is of the conclusion of a NCAA Division I soccer game, after he had cleared a ball off the goal line with seconds left to preserve a victory and put his team in the post-season conference tournament. As his teammates congratulated him, the assistant coach walked over and informed him he had given away too many passes that day and would be receiving a poor evaluation. To this day, my brother harbors anger that one of his proudest college sports memories was tarnished in that way. Beware of the coach who ignores a player's emotional state.

I do believe it is important for parents to recognize the difference between a coach who is unsafe for your child (as we mentioned above) and one who is perhaps challenging your child in a way they have not encountered in the past. I have had numerous conversations with parents who were concerned that the new coach was ruining their child's budding career. When I went to observe, what I often saw was a coach who was challenging a player who had grown comfortable with their former coach. They were now playing a new position, had a new role on the team, or were adapting to new training methods. This was not bad coaching. This was a good coach who was challenging players. There is a big difference.

Harder is not necessarily a bad thing, nor is it an unsafe thing, and pushing your child to his or her maximum can be a blessing. We often do not realize until well afterwards the benefits of being pushed and held to a higher standard by a coach or teacher. We are thankful for them today, but we were not so thankful at the time. Challenging teachers and coaches make us uncomfortable, but they also take us to a level we would never get to on our own.

Even if the coach is a difficult one, so what? We are going to have bad teachers, bad coaches, and bad bosses in our lives, so why not start early? Before you leap to the defense of your child when she is struggling to adapt to a new coach, assess the situation. Note the difference between an environment that is unsafe for your child and one that is uncomfortable. If it's the former, remove them. If it's the latter, then it is a teachable moment. Your child will thank you and the coach a little later in life.

Proper Training Environment

Youth sports should be a place where children are confronted with challenges that must be overcome, and the best coaches are always straddling the line between creating environments where players are successful and pushing the envelope to bring them out of their comfort zone and take them to the next level. If everything is a stroll in the park for your child, that is not a great learning environment. Teaching exercises and games to young children that are physically and mentally beyond their reach is not either.

Training environments for young players should allow each child to choose his own degree of difficulty. As players get older, the coach must provide a challenging environment where players can have success through great effort and focus, and then continually challenge them to get better. They should be pushed and prodded, yet the coach must also recognize when it is time to pull back. She must treat every player as an individual when assessing what motivates them and what discourages them, and apply coaching methods appropriate for each player.

When seeking an appropriate environment for your child, ask parents and evaluate firsthand if this is the case, or if there is a one-size-fits all approach to training and games. Great coaches instinctively know that every player responds differently to praise and to criticism, and they know what to dole out and when to dole it out. Bad coaches know only what worked for them as players and cannot understand why everyone does not respond the way they did.

As players progress in age and ability, there are required skill sets for each ascending level of play—thus the evolution of select and travel teams and events for the most advanced players. At this level we usually start to see the pressures of achieving successful outcomes in games and matches take their toll emotionally on players, on coaches, and on families. The substantial financial investment made by families can reach into the tens of thousands of dollars a year, and unfortunately that leads some misguided adults to judge everything by medals, trophies, and wins. This can create an environment that puts pressure on coaches and organizations to prioritize winning over development in order to keep players from jumping to the competition.

I find it sad that instead of trying to educate parents and players about development and team philosophy, many coaches choose to take the easy road and "just win baby!" To use an educational example, I cannot imagine a parent finding it acceptable for a schoolteacher to steal a copy of the state exam and have the students memorize the answers rather than teaching them algebra. In athletics, many parents find it acceptable for coaches to "cheat" their child out of her athletic education in order to win a championship. Sports are an education that for many children is just as valuable as the one they receive in the classroom. To provide them any less than an excellent one is stealing from them and is unacceptable.

How to Identify an Unsafe Environment

A safe environment for your child (or more importantly identifying an unsafe one) is easy to spot if you take the time and truly look. I'm not exactly sure how to perfectly define an unsafe environment, but to paraphrase the words of Supreme Court Justice Potter Stewart, "I know it when I see it," and you should too.

A responsible parent should do her research, talk to parents who are part of that team or club, and not just take the word of the parents of starting players. Speak to the parents whose players are at the end of the roster, who may not play as often or in crucial moments. Is the experience a great one? Are they learning? Do they love the coach? Is the organization responsive, and do they communicate their goals and expectations? Does the club have a set of core values they have adopted that they preach and model? Do they expect sports to be the centerpiece of your life or only a portion of a healthy, well-balanced childhood?

When you go to observe a game or match, ask opposing fans about the behavior of that team, watch them play, and beware of the team parent who is in charge of "recruiting" the next top player. Here are a few red flags to look out for:

- Poor sideline behavior by coaches and fans that goes unpunished by the coach/organization
- Poor behavior by players, usually on and off the field, that is neglected by the adults
- Teams with high player turnover (are they investing in and developing players, or just collecting your check until next year's crop arrives)
- Clubs with high coaching turnover
- A take-it-or-leave-it attitude by coaches, directors, and club administrators when you point out a problem
- Lack of organizational core values and principles that are written and easily accessible

There are more examples, but you get the picture. If you see attitudes and actions that do not reflect the core principles and values you want your child to learn and exemplify at school and at home, then say "Thanks, but no thanks!" These clubs may develop good players, but they rarely develop good people. If you want your child to be a good player and a good person, I can assure you there is usually another alternative out there if you keep looking. Winning is ephemeral and success is perishable, but true excellence is resilient and enduring.

Game-Changing Question for Parents

Is my child participating in a physically safe, emotionally safe, and developmentally appropriate environment, run by an organization with clearly stated core values?

Helping Your Child to Learn and Apply Life Lessons

It is up to you to help your child identify and apply the values and lessons you want them to learn from athletics. Sit down with your child and explain what these values are and why they are important. Then walk the walk, because children will listen to what we say, but more importantly they will remember what we do.

It is one thing to tell your child that the reason he is going to play sports is to learn about integrity, commitment, and determination. You must demonstrate those things. If you are screaming at coaches and referees—focused only on the match result—your actions and intentions are not congruent, and your child will remember your behavior and not your words.

Instead, use losses as teachable moments and disappointments as means to motivate your children to greater success. If you focus on bad coaching or inadequate officiating, the teachable moment is lost. Seize the moment and remind your child that "When we signed up we talked about how there would be days like today, and we wouldn't let them get us down. Remember, we promised that we would learn from these days and get better."

There are so many teachable moments in sports, not only on the field but off it as well. We can teach them about relationships, about dealing with jealousy and envy, about trying hard when others around you are not. We can teach them how to be humble in victory and graceful in defeat. We can reinforce what it means to make a commitment to a team, a coach, and an organization. We can talk about showing discipline by not attending a sleepover party the night before a big game or maintaining fitness in the off season. Perhaps most importantly, through sports we can demonstrate to our kids that life is definitely not fair, often unjust, and quite often may end in failure, but that is fine. It is how we handle this adversity that matters most.

I cannot imagine my life today without sports, for I learned many life lessons through athletics. I often draw on the inner strength I gained by overcoming injury and disappointment as an athlete to get me through tough times as an adult. In my adult life I have accomplished many difficult tasks, and I attribute those to never allowing myself to quit before I fulfilled a commitment. I remember arguing with my father about going skiing or fishing at the expense of soccer games, to which he always told me, "No, you made a commitment to this team, and when it's over you can decide if skiing or fishing is more important." I did not always appreciate that when I was seventeen, but I do now. My parents used sports to teach me important lessons and develop character, and you can do the same for your kids. They will thank you later. For as Samuel Clemens (Mark Twain) famously said:

When I was a boy of fourteen, my father was so ignorant I could hardly stand to have the old man around. But when I got to be twenty-one, I was astonished at how much the old man had learned in seven years.

Game-Changing Question for Parents
Am I helping my child to learn and apply the life lessons that sports teaches?

Action Steps for Evaluating
Proper Developmental Conditions

1. Educate yourself about athletic performance and long-term athletic development.

2. Define your core values.

3. Research sports organizations that share your values, have them written and posted, and model these values in their communication, coaching, and administration.

4. Ensure the training is developmentally appropriate and the coaches are educated and experienced at working with the age group of the children they coach.

5. Keep your eyes open and look for signs that the environment is not a safe one. Do not be fooled by wins and losses.

6. Help your child to learn and apply the life lessons the organization is teaching if they align with your core values.

7. Volunteer and give your time to organizations that are trying to do the right things. They need your help, and it is a great way to give back and help them grow.

Game-Changing Questions for Your Child

1. Is your sports experience a fun and exciting one? What makes it that way?

2. Is there anything that your coaches or any of the parents do that takes away the fun? That makes you uncomfortable?

3. Do you know what your family core values are? Do you feel your sports experience is teaching them?

4. Are your practices and games fun? Challenging? Do you feel that you are improving? In what ways?

7

Communication

The single biggest problem in communication is the illusion that it has taken place.

—George Bernard Shaw

A few years ago I coached a talented yet underperforming sixteen-year-old girl named Maria. She was incredibly inconsistent in her play and often looked very depressed and lacking in confidence. Her friends told me she often waffled about whether to continue playing or not. After trying multiple ways in training and games to help her play the way I believed she was capable of, I called her and her father in for a meeting.

Over the course of the meeting, I realized that Maria's father was the reason for her inconsistent play. He was always present at games, and many practices, and I came to realize that he was putting undue pressure on his daughter and held goals for her that did not match her reasons for playing. The biggest issue was that she was unable to communicate this with him.

After meeting with them both, I asked her dad to leave and spoke to Maria alone. For the first time she discussed with me the many issues she was unable to communicate with her dad. I then gave her some communication tips and Proactive Coaching's fantastic video "The Role of Parents in Athletics" to watch with her father. She left and I called her father back in and told him it was a requirement of his daughter's continued participation for him to watch the video with her. He agreed and they left.

Two days later, Maria showed up to training with a huge smile on her face, without her dad, and brought me back the video. "Thank you, thank you," she said. "I just had the first real conversation ever with my dad about sports, and he accepts my goals and ambitions for soccer now. I feel like a huge weight has been lifted, and I'm looking forward to playing for the first time in a long, long time." From that point forward, I coached a completely different player, one that was happy, positive, and confident. It was all because of communication.

The key to any successful parent-child or coach-child relationship is good communication. Strong communication skills are a fundamental component of raising a high-performing athlete and an essential part of keeping them in sports throughout their childhood and making them an athlete for life.

One of the oft-overlooked aspects of youth athletics is the time you are compelled to spend with your kids—and they with you—as you travel to training, games, and events. In our busy lives, we are often passing our children in the night, but sports gives you an opportunity to spend quality time together and get your kids to open up and express themselves—if you know a few secrets about communication. It is up to us to make sure that is time well spent, decide where we will actively engage our kids, and speak to them in a way that shows we are listening and we care.

When I talk to parents of older players who have moved on to college, they often consider some of their fondest memories of youth sports to be the times spent on road trips where the family was compelled to sit together and actually interact with each other. I hear others lament that because of sports they never had any time to spend with their children. When I ask them what they just did on that three-hour drive to a tournament, they say they put on a DVD for the kids or listened to the radio. These were wasted moments.

I spoke to Dr. Albert Oppedisano, author of *Education and Empowerment for the 21ˢᵗ Century Parent*, to get his advice on communication. Besides being an author and practicing psychologist, Dr. Oppedisano is part of the State of California Hostage Negotiation team, and I figure if there is anyone who knows how to speak calmly and rationally, extract information and concessions, and make sure a conversation is engaging, it has to be a hostage negotiator. Secondly, Dr. Oppedisano has spent years counseling some of California's most notorious prisoners, from death row inmates to violent offenders serving life sentences. I am quite sure that if there is anyone who wants to share their feelings less than a teenager, it is probably some of these inmates. So when Dr. Oppedisano speaks about communication, I listen. Here is what he recommends.

Be an Active Listener

First of all, become an active listener and try to understand the emotions your child is trying to express. We all know that kids, especially teenagers, love to give one- and two-word answers, which leaves adults frustrated and at times angry. If we think about it, though, we open the door to these answers by asking closed-ended questions, such as "How was practice?" This leads to those one- and two-word answers we all love: "Fine" or "Okay" or my favorite, "Eh." Instead, ask open-ended questions such as "What were three things you learned in practice today?" or "What did you work on in training today?" This requires an answer from your kids that does not allow them to shut down the conversation without it even getting started.

Paraphrase Their Main Points

Next, when your child explains a situation to you, try paraphrasing her points in your response. This will show her that you are listening and engaged; it will also allow her to correct you if you are misinterpreting what she is saying. If your daughter complains that she only plays half a game, and that the coach always lets Jenny play the whole game, responding "Why do you care how much Jenny plays?" might only shut her off and end the conversation. Responding "That coach doesn't know what she is doing" will only undermine the coach and not help you or your daughter gain any insight about the situation. Neither of these are helpful responses.

Instead, you might say "I've noticed that Jenny plays all the time. What are some of the reasons you think she gets to play more than you?" This requires an answer, tells your daughter you are listening, and may even allow your daughter to gain some new insight into the reasons she is not playing. If she makes points that are not valid, such as "She only plays a lot because she is the coach's daughter's best friend," it gives you the opportunity to educate her and make some valid points of your own. At least you will have had a conversation. At best, your daughter will see things she can do to change the situation and play more, instead of finding excuses not to improve or stop playing altogether.

Respect Their Emotions

Third, Dr. Oppedisano recommends that we use emotional labeling when we speak to our kids. Say things such as "It seems that you are angry" or "I see this upsets you." Again, it helps your child know you are listening and present, and also gives him the chance to correct you. "I'm not angry at the coach because I didn't play much," your son might say. "I'm upset because he never tells me why I don't play and what I am doing wrong."

You have allowed your son to help you understand what he is feeling and to identify the specific issue that makes him feel that way. This allows you to help him find ways to make the situation better.

Beyond this, emotional labeling gives validity to your child's feelings. We all know that children ride an emotional rollercoaster, and we often forget what a wild ride we had as kids. Note their anger, their sadness, their frustration, and give validity to their feelings in a nonjudgmental way. This lends itself to more open dialogue. If you say "I can't believe you let your coach get you so upset," you are judging their emotions and may even be interpreted by your child as criticizing his emotional state. This is especially crucial after a tough loss or a major disappointment such as getting cut from a team. If you do not acknowledge a child's emotions and just tell him to "Toughen up, it doesn't matter," you are ignoring how he feels. Quite frankly, to your child, at that moment, it does matter a great deal.

Don't Put Your Child on the Defensive

When you discuss difficult situations with your child, especially when it comes to his attitude, behavior, or effort, using "I" statements rather than "you" statements helps to foster better communication. There is a difference between stating "I feel really upset when you talk back and are disrespectful to the referee" as opposed to saying "You are really making me angry when you disrespect the referee." According to Dr. Oppedisano:

"You are" statements shut down communication and will put your child in a defensive position. You may be mad, angry, or even infuriated by your child's actions, but shutting down communication will do nothing to resolve the current conflict. "I" statements will allow you to express how you are feeling by using emotionally appropriate descriptors without blaming your child for your current mood. Owning your own emotions will also model the right way to take personal responsibility for how you feel and react to any given situation. It is crucial to remember that as rational and logical beings, we can choose how we react to other people's emotional outbursts.[17]

By using "I" instead of "You," we invite our children to take responsibility and be accountable for their actions as well as play a part in the solution.

Control Your Emotions

Another important communication technique, and perhaps the most difficult one, is controlling our emotions. As parents and coaches, we are often frustrated with our children and prone to emotional outbursts that can damage our relationship. It can be extremely difficult in a tense game to control your emotions and frustrations and still communicate with your player in an effective manner. As we all know, an angry outburst can be especially damaging to a young player.

Our words and actions are incredibly influential for the kids we care for. We must choose them wisely and unemotionally, because those words will be ingrained in the minds and hearts of our children. If you feel an emotional outburst coming from yourself or your child, take the moment to step away, breathe deeply, or even tell your child: "I am very upset right now, and I know you are as well. I'm going to take a few moments to collect myself before we speak about this. I will show you respect by not having this conversation when I am very angry, and I expect that you will show me the same respect by coming back later and having this conversation with me."

This puts the responsibility on your child to come and communicate with you, to show you respect, and to have a healthy, unemotional discussion.

Practice What You Preach

As a coach, I think often of University of North Carolina Women's Soccer Head Coach Anson Dorrance, who has won more than twenty NCAA

Division I national championships and coached legendary players such as Mia Hamm, Michelle Akers, April Heinrichs, and Kristine Lilly. He has not lost often, but when he has his players have often mentioned how his composed and unemotional responses to poor performances caught them off guard. When asked about this, Dorrance stated that if his team is losing, he begins to compose his "concession" speech about twenty minutes before the end of the game. That way, if they do lose, he has already come to grips with the loss and passed the emotional peak. He can then address his opponents, the referees, and his players unemotionally. Some might say that this is easier when you only lose two to three games a season. I say maybe it is a reason why his teams only lose two to three games a season.

Whether you are a parent or a coach, recognize that you are also a model for the children under your care. If your way to solve problems, deliver critiques, and speak to authority figures consists of emotional outbursts, then that is what you teach children to model. It always amazes me when a coach spends an entire game screaming at referees and then gets angry at the team parents or their players for doing the same. The parents should probably know better; the kids are just doing what they are shown.

Within your house, if you and your spouse always raise your voice at each other, then your kids are being told that this is the proper way to deal with conflict. If you always insult, scream, and yell at your spouse when you argue, and your spouse allows that type of treatment, how do you think your child is going to react when he or she is treated poorly? In all likelihood, your children will react exactly like your spouse. Whether you are speaking to your child about sports or to your spouse about any number of family issues, it is wise to remember that you are also teaching your children how to communicate and how to behave.

Be Consistent

Finally, be consistent in your behavior and expectations. Research shows that parents who are consistent in both discipline and expectations raise healthy and well-adjusted teenagers. The more stable and predictable your actions and reactions are, the more even-keeled your kids will be. Bad behavior that produces a harsh reaction one day should not be met with a *laissez faire* reaction the following day. Kids need to know where the boundaries are and what the consequences are for crossing them. They need consistency, and they need you to be their parent more than they need you to be their friend.

Effective communication with young athletes provides a solid foundation for them to build their emotional infrastructure. With good communication and open dialogue, you can set goals with your child and help him overcome challenges and work through issues. You become his partner and supporter throughout his athletic journey. He will know that his emotions are valid, his opinions are respected, and that you love him, care for him, and are present. He will also be able to tell you when to take a step back and let it be his career, not yours.

Without open and honest communication with your children, it is very difficult to know their dreams and ambitions. Forget helping them to reach their goals. Become a better communicator and model good communication skills. Strong relationships are built upon these skills. Provide your kids with consistency and stability, and then allow and encourage them to have an opinion. That puts you on the road to raising a happy, high-performing young athlete.

Game-Changing Activity for Parents

Take some time and think about how you communicate, not only with your children, but with your spouse, friends, and other adults. Remember you are modeling communication for your children. Are you modeling the skills you want them to possess?

Action Steps for
Improved Communication with Your Children

1. Take advantage of the opportunity sports gives you to spend time with your children.
2. Be an active listener.
3. In conversation, try paraphrasing their main points so they know you are listening.
4. Respect and understand your child's emotions.
5. Do not put your children on the defensive; use "I" instead of "you" statements.
6. Control your emotions, and know when to step away from a conversation.
7. Model positive, unemotional communication with your spouse and other family members.
8. Be consistent in your behavior and expectations.

Game-Changing Questions for Your Child

1. When we talk do I respect your emotions? Do you think I am listening?
2. Do I always act the way that I ask you to behave? If not, can you give some examples?
3. Am I consistent in my reactions to certain situations?
4. How can we work together to ensure that you and I are on the same page when it comes to sports?
5. Do you feel like you can talk to me about sports?

8

Control

I should probably tell you I support my son's tennis because he gets so much out of it, that it improves him mentally and physically and teaches him so much about life. All that is certainly true, but the real reason is because it adds drama to my life.

—Letter from an anonymous tennis mom to writer Emily Greenspan, "Little Winners," *New York Times Magazine*, April 26, 1981

mily was a talented young soccer player in a club I ran. She enjoyed the game, had great friends on her team, and loved her coach. Unfortunately, her parents wanted Emily to move to an advanced team and did not feel the need to ask her what she wanted. Their intentions, motivation, and love for their daughter were good, but they failed to recognize that not only did their daughter not want to play on that team, but she had no friends there and was much happier on the

116

lower-level team. Emily was a good player, with an incredibly positive self-image as the best player on the B team, but in her new environment she lost confidence and thought less of herself because she had no control over her placement. This was not a recipe for high performance.

The problem in Emily's situation was not necessarily that her parents wanted to encourage her to participate at a higher level, or face a bigger challenge. The basic problem was that her parents wanted to push her toward their goals for her and not her own. They never bothered to give her any control over the circumstances and challenges she was faced with. By not choosing her challenge, she never embraced or accepted it. Instead of striving confidently and positively toward a new experience that she had asked for, she was reluctantly forced to accept it. She eventually allowed herself to be defined by her new circumstances and perceived lesser value on the new team. Emily ended up quitting soccer because she had no control over her experience.

One of the scariest parts of becoming a parent and watching your child grow up is ceding control as they get older. We spend so many years overseeing every meal, every nap, and every activity, but as they get older we begin to let go. We know that our kids are constantly fighting to gain some semblance of control over their lives, and always pushing the boundaries and testing the waters to learn what is acceptable and what is not. As parents, we accept (sometimes grudgingly) that we have to continuously grant them more control as time goes on.

Our children also want a degree of control over which new experiences and challenges they bring into their lives, who they hang out with, and how they view and present themselves to the world (i.e., dress, haircut, makeup). As they mature, they undergo a process of shedding their childhood image and attributes and creating their own young adult persona. It can be a constant battle for parents and a great place to teach compromise.

If your child is going to be a high performer, he needs control over his athletic experience. The sport must be his choice, his performance must be based upon his efforts and motivation, and his development must be a result of his failures and successes. As a result, the outcome of his achievement belongs to him and him alone. With control, children take ownership of their activity and responsibility for the process of achievement, and they learn to value it because it belongs to them.

Children who are given control over their sports experience are more likely to become high performers because they embrace the process of attaining excellence, rather than any outcomes that are a result of their hard work. Their focus on effort and enjoyment supersedes any need for medals and trophies. They can define themselves in their own self-image (I am a hustler, I am creative, I am energetic, I am a great teammate). Children in control usually practice more deliberately and more often. They focus longer and demonstrate interest outside of practice. They seek out additional opportunities to hone their craft. They do not make excuses for failure, for they recognize that the only things they control are their efforts. In a nutshell, they take pride in their work.[18]

Many parents deny control of the sports experience to their children. They select what they play, where they play, who they play with, and why they are playing in the first place. Then they wonder why their children push back, complain when it's time to practice, and do not put forth sufficient effort and commitment to improve. It is because they have been denied any ownership in the activity. They have no control.

Can you see how this does not produce better athletes? Though sometimes playing up a year or on a better team can be beneficial, it often produces bitter athletes who quit the game they so recently loved. Without control, children will not take responsibility for a new challenge. On the other hand, when you grant them some modicum of control, you will see children who define commitment and rise to new challenges with confidence, courage, and a positive state of mind that is conducive to high achievement.

Let Your Kids Go

Once you are confident that your child is in a safe and developmentally appropriate environment, one of the most important things you will ever do as the parent of a young athlete is to let them go and let their sports experience belong to them. The phrase I like to use with parents I learned from Proactive Coaching founder Bruce Brown, a longtime coach and advocate for responsible parenting. He calls it "releasing your child to the game." We have a saying in coaching that everything has been tried before, and good coaches steal from other good coaches, so you might as well borrow the best stuff from everyone you know. The first time I ever heard Coach Brown speak, I knew I would be borrowing a lot of stuff from him.[19]

I asked Coach Brown what the biggest change was that he had seen in his years as a coach, educator, author, and speaker. He did not hesitate when he answered: "Youth sports has gone from a peer-controlled activity to an adult-controlled one. They are told what to wear, where to stand, and what to do. Kids never get to play anymore; they are always performing for adults."

In asking parents to "release your child to the game," Coach Brown implores us to accept that the sports your child plays are his and his alone, not yours. We did not win the game, he did. We did not strike out ten batters, she did. Once you release your children to the game, once you let the sport belong to them, then their accomplishments belong to them. This allows you to accept your role as spectator at games and give them control of the outcome. You will rise above the emotional frustration and anger that many parents feel when their child or his team is unsuccessful in a match. When you release your child, you also release yourself from your own anxiety and angst, and your child's athletic experience will be better for both of you.

Perhaps more importantly, by releasing your child you remove any chance that your child believes he is responsible for your happiness. This may sound like a silly thought, but look around at your next athletic event. Look for the angry and disappointed parent faces on the losing side. Despite what they say, their actions are telling their children that the outcome of the game determines their happiness. This is an incredible burden to place upon a child, whether it is intended or not. It is not a recommended path if you want your child to be a high performer.

There are ways to make sure you have released your child, and you are not depending upon your child for happiness. Here's how.

Game-Changing Question for Parents

Have I released my child and given him/her control and ownership of the sports experience?

Setting Goals with Your Child

One of the most powerful things you can do for your child is to recognize his goals and reasons for playing a sport. Bad things happen when a child's goals and his parents' goals are incompatible. This is a recipe for disaster. While parents can help their child see the big picture and develop proper goals, we must accept that our child may not have the same purpose for playing that we ascribe to him. If we try to force our goals upon him, he will never take ownership of the experience. We must accept our child's goals.

At this point it is crucial to understand the difference between goals and expectations, for many children grow up feeling guilty and unworthy for never meeting their parents' expectations. Goals are possible accomplishments that may or may not be achieved, yet can provide satisfaction to children just by going through the process of setting them and trying to attain them. Expectations, on the other hand, are all or nothing; they are assumptions of achievement. The difference is subtle but very important, for both are important tools when it comes to raising high performers. We should place expectations upon our children and set goals for them, but we need to make sure that each tool is used properly.

We should place certain expectations upon our children, but these must be things within their control. We can expect them to be courteous, committed, honest, caring, responsible, and a host of other things we would agree are important. These are expectations based upon effort and values. They must be clearly communicated, and the consequences for failing to meet them should be equivalent with each expectation and consistently applied. Your child has the ability to be all of these things, and if he is not then he should expect that there will be consequences. It is okay for us to be disappointed in him for not meeting our clear expectations, and we should hold our children to high standards that reflect our values and beliefs.

All too often, though, parental expectations become *ability* (you will win because you are the best) and *outcome* (I know you will win) oriented, and become confused with our goals for our children. When we expect them to win a game, we are expecting them to accomplish something that is not completely within their control. They may give their best effort and still lose. If a child believes that a parent's love is tied to the expectation of winning, and he does not win, he may believe that he is less loved or valued. This creates anxiety and inhibits performance. High performers have expectations placed upon them, but only upon things that are fully within their control.[20]

Goals, on the other hand, are possible outcomes, but process oriented. We should help our children to recognize and set two types of goals: *process* goals and *forward-moving* goals. Process goals are related to things within our control, and forward-moving goals are related to our dreams. Both are important.

When we speak about process goals, we are talking about goals that focus on the journey and not the outcome. An outcome goal is usually nonspecific and out of our control, such as "I want to be a professional basketball player" or "I want to win state." It is ambitious, it may be worthy, but it is out of our control.

Process goals are doing all the things that get you to a destination. "I am going to practice on my own for thirty minutes a day." "I am going to attend one extra practice a week with another team." "I am going to quit eating sweets and lose two pounds a week for the next three months." These goals are SMART (specific, measurable, attainable, realistic, and timely), and your child can see and measure progress week to week, month to month.

Process goals are also great because they are entirely within a child's control. An outcome goal such as "win state" may sound great, but think of all the things outside of her control that can affect the outcome. Her opponents, her teammates, her coach, the officials, the weather, injuries, acts of God—all these things can play a role in inhibiting the fulfillment of that goal. She can do everything in her power to win state, but numerous factors outside her control can derail that dream. Instead, by focusing on process goals, she is fully in control of the results and often will achieve outcome goals as a byproduct of her effort.

Forward-moving goals are the far-reaching dreams that I believe all children should have. They are hard to measure, at times not very specific, and rarely timely, but they are crucial to energize children and let their imagination soar. Kids should strive to win state or play in the NBA, and we should encourage these larger, energizing goals. That said, we should also help our children focus on the process, for without accomplishing those goals our forward-moving goals rarely come to fruition.

I was well into my coaching career before I truly recognized the importance of goal setting, as well as the importance of the role of parents in the process. When I did, I began to require each of my players and their parents to fill out similar questionnaires in the preseason. I asked the players to complete five simple statements:

1. Three ways I am an asset to my team are …
2. My role on the team is …
3. Three things I want to improve on are …
4. Three individual goals for this season are …
5. Three team goals for this season are …

At the same time I provided the parents with a similar list of tasks to complete:

1. List three things your son/daughter does well already as a player.
2. What is your child's role on this team?
3. List three things you would like to see them improve upon.
4. List three individual goals you have for your son/daughter.
5. List three goals you have for the team this season.

I asked the players and parents to fill these out on their own and then to sit down and compare notes. What I discovered was that the players and parents who shared the same goals and ambitions often had a great relationship. They were on the same page as to why they were participating in sports, and thus the parents understood the levels of commitment and effort their children were putting forth. Those kids were usually the high performers on the team.

As for the families where there was no compatibility or middle ground between players and parents, I often saw strife and poor performance from the players and anger, frustration, and a feeling of "I'm wasting my money" from the parents. The biggest divide for parents and players was usually regarding the player's role on the team and the parents' goals for their child. The players often were very realistic about their expected contribution based upon their current abilities and those of their teammates. Many parents, on the other hand, saw a much more significant role for their child, usually based upon what kind of player they thought their child should be rather than what he currently was.

The child's goals often aligned with their effort, commitment, and ability. The parents' goals aligned with the athlete they wished they had instead of the one they did.

Parents need to accept their child's goals if they want their child to have control over their sports experience. If your goals for your daughter this season are to get a college scholarship, make the national select team, and score thirty goals, while your daughter wants to have fun, play with friends, and stay in shape, that abyss will swallow your relationship with her. You must accept her goals. While you may counsel her on aiming higher, you cannot force your goals to be hers when they are this far apart. I have seen many a vast expanse between parent and child goals in my teams, and in every case where the parents could not give up their own goals and accept their child's, it ended badly for the child and the family.

If your child is older and you are paying a substantial amount of money for their participation, you are well within your rights as a parent to decide that $10,000 a year for travel soccer is not a wise investment for a player who is only looking to hang out with her friends, go to half the practices, and make a minimal effort. It is up to you to communicate that to her and let her know that while you support her participation on this particular team, she could get the same benefits out of another, less expensive team, and the family could use the money for a trip or a college fund. There is nothing wrong with telling your child that certain teams have certain expectations, and if their goals do not meet these expectations, it is not a good fit. Usually, though, as highly talented players get older, peer pressure results in them making this decision on their own, for they are no longer willing to put in the time and effort it takes to stay competitive with teammates who are more ambitious and invested than they are.

Many times I had parents list individual goals such as "work hard," "be competitive," "learn sportsmanship," and so on, while their son would list things such as "score twenty goals" and "learn to kick with my left foot." These are both excellent sets of goals, and I think it's great that the parent in this case sees the larger perspective for their child. In this case, the parents never communicated to their child about the importance of the process goals and value goals that would eventually lead to things like scoring goals and learning specific techniques. It is up to you as a parent to speak to your child, to help him see the big picture, and teach him that successful outcomes are usually the result of good process goals. Kids will usually grasp that concept pretty quickly.

As a coach, I also learned not to set my own team and individual player goals until I read the goal-setting answers from the players. I did so because it is crucially important for players and teams to commit in writing to everything they want out of a season. That way they can be held accountable for their performance, their attitude, and their effort in training and games. After I compiled the results from my survey, I would sit the team down and tell them how many of them wanted to win a state championship, or qualify for nationals, or play in college, or do an extra practice a week. Then, each and every day in training, I would remind them that if the effort and concentration were not at the level they had agreed upon, their actions and intentions were not compatible at the moment. By giving them complete ownership in the team ambitions, I gave them total accountability for fulfilling them. This usually led to player development, team development, and a unit that invested in a goal, an idea, and a vision for their season. We did not always get there, but at least we always knew where we were trying to go.

Start with Three Simple Goals

Every child is different, and every child should have their own specific process and forward-moving goals. That being said, parents often ask me where to start the process of goal setting. I believe that every child, no matter what age or ability, can have the following three sport-specific goals:

Have Fun: If your child is not having fun, he will eventually quit. He has little chance of becoming a high performer and will never take true ownership of his activity. By letting him know you support his goal of having fun, you greatly improve your chances of making the sporting experience a positive one for your child.

Work Hard: Effort is completely within your child's control. Whether it is in games, practices, or preseason preparation, your child should set to a goal of working hard each and every time he steps on the field.

Be Committed: When you make the decision to register a child for a sport, it should be understood that barring any dangerous, unforeseen circumstances he should be committed to meeting or exceeding the expectations of the sport in training, games, travel, etc. If one day he says "I don't want to go to practice today" it is a great chance to remind him that he committed to a ten-week season, and he has a few weeks to go.

By guiding your child in the establishment of these three goals, he can take ownership over his activity. As he becomes more involved and grows in competence, you can then start to set specific and performance-related goals. I do not believe there is any age too young to help your child understand that you want him to have fun, work hard, and be committed. By starting young, you will teach him important values, and these three goals will provide a solid foundation upon which to build a high achiever.

Game-Changing Activity for Parents

If you have not already done so, do some goal setting with your child. Both of you can set three personal and three team goals (if applicable), and then compare to see if you are on the same page. If needed, guide him in setting the three goals of fun, effort, and commitment, and then accept your child's goals.

How to Push Your Child

One of the most difficult situations we encounter as adults is determining when to give our kids a push in the right direction, and when to back off and accept their decisions or their inaction. A push at the right time can be the springboard to high achievement and happiness. A push at the wrong time, in the wrong way, may lead to disappointment and resentment from your child. One thing is for certain, though. It is our job as parents to push our children when they become complacent, to urge them to keep trying when they are unsuccessful at first, and to help propel them through times of difficulty when we know achievement is just around the corner.

We become a valuable ally to our child once we understand where we should push them and when and how to push them. Learning the where, when, and how is crucial, for just as an ill-timed comment or an emotional response can be damaging to a child, so can parents who push their kids too hard or do not push at all. Two of the leading authorities in the sports parenting field, Dr. Dan Gould and Dr. Jim Taylor, give some great insight into this difficult dilemma that we all must face.

Dr. Dan Gould of Michigan State University calls this adult intervention the "optimal push." Optimal push refers to prodding kids based upon the core values they have selected to pursue, and the goals they have agreed to strive for. When they say "I want to play in college," then as a coach or parent it is your responsibility to make sure they don't sleep in and skip practice, or quit, or not commit fully. It is not your job to make them do what they never said they wanted to do, but it is your job to remind them of THEIR commitments and goals which THEY came up with. As Dr. Gould describes it, optimal push is telling your child "If you want to do it, then do it right!"

There is obviously a fine line here, and it is a line that both coaches and parents constantly dance along. Dr. Gould's research on elite young tennis players demonstrated that at the middle school age, nearly every player considered quitting at some point. Of course, many persevered and became very talented and successful players. There was clearly a coach, a parent, or both who provided that small nudge that got them over the hump and helped them overcome their lack of confidence, poor commitment, or whatever else was holding them back. The push is clearly a necessity, but how do we make sure it is a positive one?

Dr. Jim Taylor, in his book *Positive Pushing*, encourages parents to take an active and vigorous role in their child's upbringing. He asserts that parents have three essential roles: act in their child's best interests, develop a loving relationship with their child, and promote his or her happiness, development, and growth into adulthood. By activating our children's self-esteem, giving them ownership, and helping them to master their emotions, we can positively push them to do things that they do not believe they are capable of.

"Kids are basically creatures of inertia," says Dr. Taylor. "They'll tend to stay in one place unless somebody says, 'You can do a little more. You can do a little better.' One of the great things about being pushed is it's immensely satisfying. One of the great joys in life is setting a goal, working toward a goal, and achieving a goal. And if kids can learn that, then they're going to be achievement-oriented. They're going to strive to become as successful as they can. Plus they're going to get great joy and satisfaction out of it."

Dr. Taylor cautions us to do this within a loving and caring environment, where our children do not tie their performance to our love for them. We must be aware of the red flags that we are pushing them in a negative way, such as taking credit for their achievement or taking ownership of our children's sports. Most importantly, we must push our kids on things they have control over—process goals—rather than focusing solely on successful outcomes. Kids can control their effort, their commitment, their diligence, and their emotions, and as parents if we focus our pushing on those areas we will not strain our relationship with them.[21]

This is where building a strong communication foundation comes in. With open and honest dialogue, proper goal setting, and a partnership between the coaches, parents, and athletes, adults can create the opportunity to have an opinion and give input on whether a child's effort and commitment is sufficient in a given situation.

Ultimately, if you believe that your child needs a push in the right direction, then decide upon the goals in collaboration with her. Give her some control over where she is headed, and guide her based upon your adult experience. Give her a choice, let her select her goals, and then work together to achieve those goals. Make the goals process-oriented. Don't do it for her, don't consistently nag her and remind her of her shortcomings, and don't judge every performance along that path as an inadequate step to the ultimate goal. This will just frustrate your child. Instead, support her on the journey, and every day demonstrate through your words and actions that you love her, you believe in her ultimate success, and you value the effort she is putting into the task.

As difficult as it may be sometimes, it is our responsibility as adults to let players know where they stand ability-wise and what they are capable of. This does not preclude them from being great athletes and teammates, or from becoming high performers. It also does not give them false hopes and dreams when what they really need is perspective from you. If you are unsure, ask a coach who will tell you the truth about your child. You would not encourage your C-minus student to apply to Yale, and you should not try to convince your average athlete that college recruiters are about to come knocking at your door. Sport offers so much more than this, so be honest and your children will appreciate you for it.

That said, I also believe we should encourage kids to have ambitious goals and extraordinary dreams. We must help them adjust and evaluate these goals as their season and their career progresses. There is nothing wrong with asking a player "Why do you only want to score ten goals this season? I think you are capable of scoring twenty if you stay healthy and work hard." Coaches can ask a team "Why don't you guys think we can win state? We only lost by a goal to the top team last year, and we were right there. If we work a little harder and do a few things differently, we can win." Boom, the light goes on, players are empowered by the confidence of their coach or parent, and then their goals begin to morph with higher expectations. It is a fine line between imposing your own goals and encouraging your children to dream a little bigger, and when you can successfully navigate that line, that is where the most achievement takes place.

In a nutshell, when it comes to goal setting, there is only one way to do it. AIM HIGH! To paraphrase Bob Ballard, when asked why he takes on such large projects as searching for the *Titanic*, if you climb and fall off a 500-foot mountain you are toast, and if you climb and fall off a 25,000-foot mountain you are toast. Since the consequences are similar, you might as well climb the big mountain and achieve something really incredible. The same goes for goals. Be ambitious, temper that with a dose of realism, and help your athlete aim higher than he would on his own. If your child wants to aim for the stars, so what? Tell him to make sure his actions match his dreams, and he may hit the moon on the way out!

Game-Changing Question for Parents
Am I pushing my child toward his/her goals or toward my own?

The Ride Home and the Post-Game Talk
Numerous researchers have asked athletes of all ages and abilities what was their least favorite sports moment, and their answer was nearly unanimous: after the game and the conversation on the ride home. Emotions are high, disappointment, frustration, and exhaustion are heightened for both player and parent, yet many parents choose this moment to confront their child about a play, criticize them for having

a poor game, and chastise their child, their teammates, their coach, and their opponents. There could not be a less teachable moment in your child's sporting life than the ride home.

One of the biggest problems on the ride home is that a simple question from you, often meant to encourage your own child, can be construed as an attack on a teammate or coach by your child. Our kids do not need us to question their actions or those of their teammates or coaches in the emotional moments after games. A simple comment such as "Why does Jenny get all the shots?" may be meant to imply that you think she is a good shooter who should also take shots, but it is interpreted by your daughter as meaning "Jenny is a ball hog!" Questions such as "Why does Billy always play goalie?" or "Why does your team always play zone?" can just as easily undermine the coach's authority and again cause confusion and uncertainty for your child.

Many children have indicated that parental actions and conversations after games made them feel as though their value and worth was tied to their athletic performance and the wins and losses of their team. Ask yourself whether you are quieter after a hard loss, or happier and more buoyant after a big win. Do you tend to criticize and dissect your child's performance after a loss but overlook many of the same mistakes because she won? If you see that you are doing this, even though your intentions may be well-meaning, your child's perceptions of your words and actions can be quite detrimental to her performance and to your relationship.

Parents need to be a source of confidence and comfort in all situations, such as when your child has played well in a loss, when your child has played poorly, and especially when your child has played very little or not at all. Even then, it is critically important that you do not bring the game up for them, as uninvited conversations may cause resentment. Give kids the time and space to digest the game and recover physically and emotionally from a match. When your child is ready to bring the game up and talk about it, be a quiet and reflective listener, and make sure she can see the big picture and not just the outcome of a single event. Help her work through the game, and facilitate her growth and education by guiding her toward her own answers. Kids learn a lot when they realize things such as "we had a bad week of practice and coach told us this was coming." If you need to say something, tell them how much you enjoy watching them play.

The only exception to the above "ride home" rule is when your child engages in behavior that you would not accept at home, such as spitting, cursing, assaulting an opponent, or disrespecting a coach or authority figure. In these cases you should initiate the conversation, not as a parent to an athlete, but as a parent to a child. Even then you must be careful and considerate of the emotions of the match and choose your words wisely. Deal with the issue and then put it to bed; do not use it as a segue to a discussion of the entire game.

Game-Changing Questions for Parents

Do I initiate discussion of the game on the ride home? How does my child react to these discussions? Is he an active participant, or is he reluctant to speak about it?

Recognizing if You Have Not Released Your Child

Below is a checklist from Bruce Brown that identifies a few simple actions and phrases that you might catch yourself saying, or doing, that demonstrate that you have not released your child to the game. Are you, or a parent you know, displaying any of the following behaviors?

- Living your personal athletic dreams through your child
- Sharing credit for your child's successes, i.e., "We struck out ten batters today" or "I showed him that move!"
- Trying to solve all your child's sports-related problems, always calling the coach to "sort it out," instead of teaching your child

how to communicate with his coach, his teammates, etc. Have you given your child the responsibility to be the problem solver?

- Still trying to coach your child even though he knows more about the game than you do
- Feeling nervous and anxious before games, depressed after defeats, and making mental coaching notes during the game to provide advice afterwards
- Your child avoiding you after games, or showing signs he is embarrassed by your presence and involvement

There is a very fine line between under-involvement and over-involvement, and we are often tiptoeing along that line throughout our child's athletic career. Sometimes we push when we should be pulling. This is okay as long as we are able to recognize when that happens and make appropriate changes. Please take a look at some of the warning signs above, and ask yourself if you partake in any of them. If the answer is yes, try taking a step back and releasing your child to their game. Without releasing them to the game, high performance and happiness begin to diminish. Kids need control, and you are the one who can give it to them.

Action Steps for Giving Your Child Control

1. Reflect on whether you have let your child go:
   a. Are my emotions tied to wins and losses?
   b. Do I coach on the ride home?
   c. Do I model good behavior?
   d. Do I take credit for my child's accomplishments?
2. Help your child to set process goals that are SMART (specific, measurable, attainable, realistic, timely). Encourage them to think big!
3. Accept your child's goals.

4. Push your child when their actions are not matching their goals.

5. Do not push your child to achieve things that are in your best interest.

Game-Changing Questions for Your Child

1. Why do you play sports?

2. What are your goals for playing?

3. Do you feel like I push you too hard? Not enough? Do you know why I push you?

4. How can I give you more control over your sports experience?

9

Competence

They are able because they think they are able.

—Virgil

Tryouts were always my least favorite part of running elite-level soccer programs. It was always a time when many kids had their dreams shattered, were overcome with disappointment, and were ready to quit. One such athlete was Zach, a small yet exceedingly talented player who was devastated that he was put on the club's second tier team and not the top one.

Zach's parents asked me to meet with him, for he told them he was ready to quit soccer. In the meeting, I explained to him that while he was technically and tactically ready to take the next step, I was worried that his physical stature would not allow him to use his skill and guile. I was worried that going from the top player on the second team to the sixteenth player on our top team was not the right move for him at that time. I explained to him that in one year he would be ready, for he would catch up physically, and then his ability would shine through.

Thankfully, after our talk, and because of his loving and sensible parents, Zach stuck it out on the second team for another season. The next year, he was selected to the top team and quickly established himself as a top player. Three years later, he was the starting central midfielder on a top ACC Men's Soccer team as a freshman! All he needed was the patience to develop competence in all aspects of his game and an environment that allowed him to do so.

Parents understand that learning involves being confronted with tasks that children are unable to do at first. We also know that with proper encouragement and a little trial and error, they will eventually find success. Once they gain skill, they feel competent. Our role is to help our kids understand the learning process and to employ a few simple steps that preserve their motivation to learn and their ability to acquire skill. Competence is a characteristic of all high performers. In order to help our children attain competence, we must:

1. Define exactly what competence is
2. Understand the role of competition in gaining competence
3. Explore a powerful theory of gaining and teaching competence
4. Recognize whether relative age pertains to your child, and affects his performance
5. Help your child overcome disappointment by both making him feel better and be better

The Definition of Competence

Competence is the belief in ourselves that we are capable of taking on any challenge, any task, confident in our ability to succeed and willing to learn what is needed to achieve. Brendon Burchard, bestselling author and performance expert, defines competence as "our ability to understand, successfully perform in, and master our world." Experts in the fields of psychology and human performance have found that our competence level determines the tasks we choose to undertake, the items and activities we choose to give attention to, and the effort we put into those things. It determines our levels of adaptability and resiliency and oftentimes whether we choose to lead or follow. Competence and confidence go hand-in-hand; the more competent we are, the more confidence we have in our performance. And the more confident we are, the more likely we are to seek out ways to become more competent.[22]

Children are some of the most resilient creatures, especially when they are in an environment where they are unafraid to initially lack competence. They will try and fail and try again. As I tell the kids I coach, "Don't say I can't; say I will try." And they do. Once they get it right, the smile on their face and the confidence in their voice beams across the field. "Coach, were you watching? I got it!" Whereas most adults shy away from things they know they cannot do, for fear of embarrassing themselves or getting hurt, children can almost always be convinced to give it a try. If the activity is appropriate, they will eventually get it.

Competence is an essential component of self esteem and confidence. By becoming competent, children learn that their actions matter. This reinforces a sense of control and mastery in their life and reminds them that they have the abilities needed to be successful in whatever they are pursuing. Once they have some success, they are not afraid to challenge themselves, to go beyond their current level and try to attain an even higher one.

Children who feel competent will naturally seek out additional challenges and find ways to test themselves, confident that success will happen again because they have already succeeded. They will approach learning with enthusiasm and pleasure and not see it as a painful process. If they are made aware, asked to be mindful of their successes, and not allowed to dwell on their failures, then they will associate their activity with achievement, happiness, and fun. If you couple this learning with real goals, set timetables, and initiate a plan of action, then get kids to buy into that plan by helping them see the value it has for their own lives, you will have a stable of high performers who are confident and eager to learn.

When parents are overprotective of their children, they eliminate opportunities for children to gain competence, confidence, and control in their lives. Children who are never allowed to have either success or failure do not learn to take responsibility for their actions, nor do they accept the consequences for those actions. They do not develop the skills needed to achieve certain outcomes they are trying to attain. They also never learn that their parents love them unconditionally, regardless of whether they succeed or fail. As a result, they never learn to manage the inevitable challenges and disappointments that happen on the road to achievement, and this sets them up for many troubling issues later in life.

Dr. Jim Taylor argues that parents need to allow their children to develop two aspects of belief in order to attain competence: global belief and specific belief. Global belief refers to a child's universal confidence that his actions matter and that he has the ability to overcome challenges, while specific belief pertains to a child's perceived competence in a distinct activity.

By establishing global belief in himself, a child learns the crucial correlation between effort and outcome and takes ownership over his achievements. He learns to earn success. Without global belief as part of his identity, a child may begin to believe that his success is due to his ability and not his effort. This often happens in young athletes who are top performers early on because they are talented, older, grew a bit faster, and thus had success. Yet when these "big fish" move to the bigger pond, their talent can only take them so far, as they are surrounded by equally talented individuals. High-performing athletes recognize that *only their talent combined with their effort* will lead them to the next level. Those who do not recognize this usually fizzle out and quit sports.

Children who develop global belief are more apt to become competent and develop specific belief in the activities they undertake. Confident in their ability to master tasks, and cognizant of the effort needed to do so, children will undertake specific athletic, academic, and other types of challenges. They will assume control over their experience and not be afraid of small setbacks. They will often push back against a parent who is intruding too much upon their activity, however well-intentioned the parent might be. We must recognize this and allow our kids to chart their own course. We must allow our children to face all the positives and negatives that come with achievement, from successes to failures, and from joy to disappointment. Only then will a child truly acquire the strong self-belief needed to continuously succeed.

Ultimately, our children need both types of belief to achieve competence. Children may become incredibly successful in certain sports or activities, but without the necessary universal belief in themselves they can feel very inadequate outside of those activities. They can become over-reliant on their athletic, academic, or musical achievement for their own self-esteem, and thus an injury or failure can become devastating to all aspects of their life. They may view their value as intrinsically linked with their achievement in a specific activity; when it is gone, as it inevitably will be, they may no longer see any value in their lives. This type of competence does not serve children well. Parents must ensure that their child's competence in sports is built upon their belief in themselves outside of the sport, and not the other way around.[23]

The Games Do Matter but Not How You Think

Sport-specific competence is developed through deliberate, focused practice. It should be enjoyable, but it also needs to be repetitive to develop proper muscle memory and mylenate the nervous system to make sport-specific activities habit. During the skill-sensitive periods we spoke about in our discussion of LTAD, children need to train extensively. Yet all too often it is during these sensitive times that children are introduced to select and travel sports, and parents turn their attention toward competition and away from training. Nothing could be more harmful to a young athlete's development than this.

It is important to remind ourselves that the purpose of competition for young athletes is to gain additional skill mastery, not to win trophies or championships. Games are additional training opportunities; they just happen to be against unfamiliar opponents. They have higher intensity and usually more competitiveness, and therefore they can be even better than practice because the learning opportunities—and the chances to fail and then overcome failure—are more frequent.

In soccer, for example, at the highest levels a player might possess the ball for 90-120 seconds of a 90-minute game. LTAD tells us that the preteen years are crucial for skill development. Now if you signed your kid up for my team, and in a 90-minute training session I ran him without a ball for 88 minutes and then let him touch the ball for 2 minutes, you would ask for your money back. When we emphasize competition over training for our young players, we are essentially doing just that.

The games matter because they teach tactics, positioning, and focus, but in terms of skill development, that is done on the training field. We need to do more of it. So next time you sign your child up for travel soccer, instead of asking how many tournaments you get to go to, ask what is the ratio between training and games. That is what your money is supposed to be paying for.

Game-Changing Question for Parents

What role does competition play in my child's athletic development? Is it benefiting my child, or hindering his/her development?

The Slanty Line Theory

One of the best ways adults can help children build competence is by using the slanty line theory of teaching, developed by Dr. Muska Mosston. The slanty line theory is a concept that refutes the traditional method of teaching all kids the same thing, at the same time. Think about the old broomstick game of high-water low-water, where a stick starts low to the ground where all the kids can jump over it. As the stick is slowly raised, children begin to be eliminated from the competition until there is only one winner. You can see why this method is counterproductive in the development of young children, since the ones that need the activity the most are eliminated first.

If you take the stick and slant it so that one end is lower than the other, children who want to run and jump and feel successful can do so at their own pace. When the players feel comfortable they will seek new challenges. Players can participate at their own level. They can attain the aforementioned state of "flow"—the balance between challenge and accomplishment that brings total focus and satisfaction.

The slanty line also allows children of all levels to play together, which is the essence of youth sports. Given the right opportunities, children will naturally seek out challenges and take risks; they will not continue activities in which they are continually and easily eliminated or wait to take turns. Each child is measured against his own previous best, not against other teammates.

Five-year-olds come in all shapes and sizes, as a five-year-old born in January is very different from a five-year-old born the following December, so comparing the abilities of kids of the same chronological age (even though one of them may be 20 percent older than the other) is not always fair or realistic (more about this issue below). Using the slanty line approach to learning, each child can succeed at their own pace, and in their own way.

Think about the child who believes he is incompetent, or less competent, than his peers. This is the child that is often compared, and compares himself, with peers who are bigger, faster, stronger, and perhaps more skillful than he is, and he focuses on what he *cannot* do instead of what he *can* do. Because he always comes up short when measured against his teammates, he is not confident of his ability to perform, nor does he become an avid learner, ready to take on new things, put himself in difficult situations, and rise to new challenges. He is the child who doesn't raise his hand when asked to demonstrate, and doesn't want to go into the tie game, afraid he will mess it up for everyone else.

This boy's confidence is tied to his perceived lack of competence in comparison to the kids around him. Sadly, many times in the classroom and on the athletic field, the factors creating his lesser ability might be well beyond his control. He might be a year younger, a foot shorter, and thirty pounds lighter than his teammates. He may compete against kids that are bigger, faster, and stronger than him, and perhaps even mentally and emotionally ahead of him. These things usually even out as kids get older, but unfortunately, for many children, it is already too late.

Relative Age and the Outlier Effect

In his book *Outliers: The Story of Success*, Malcolm Gladwell analyzes the correlation between arbitrary age cutoffs in sports and schools and the statistically high success ratio of kids with birthdates within a few months of those cutoffs. He discusses the work of Canadian psychologist Roger Barnsley, who in the 1980s first drew attention to the story of relative age in youth hockey players. Barnsley noticed that an extraordinary number of elite youth and professional hockey players had birthdays in January, February, and March. In the Ontario Junior Hockey league, nearly five times as many players were born in January than November. This held true for elite eleven- to thirteen-year-olds and again for players in the NHL!

He eventually discovered that in any group of elite hockey players, 40 percent will have been born between January and March, 30 percent between April and June, 20 percent between July and September, and

10 percent between October and December! Is it the least bit surprising to know that the age eligibility cutoff for Canadian junior hockey is January 1?

One of our biggest problems in youth sports, and early education for that matter, is that we have institutionalized and streamlined our registration protocols into yearlong time blocks. We organize children chronologically instead of developmentally. While this certainly makes it easy to organize and segregate classes and teams, it puts our preadolescent children (ages five to thirteen) into situations where some may have a head start, or be denied one, because of birth month. Sure, two kids may be five years old, but there may be eleven months of additional development for the child born in January. That difference can be huge at this age and affect them for the rest of their lives.

The problem lies with how and when we segregate our elite athletes and students. We do this at a very young age, often five or six in school, and nine or ten in athletics. We then take those "top" athletes and give them the best facilities, the best coaching, more opportunities, better teammates to play with, and stronger opponents to play against. In schools we send them to gifted classes and give them extra tutoring to help foster their "higher" intelligence and make sure they are not bored.

Perhaps most importantly, we demonstrate to them with our words and actions that they are better than their peers because they have been selected for this opportunity based upon their ability. We tell them they are smarter than their classmates, and they are good at what they do. As all educators and coaches know, if you want your students and athletes to perform their best, you must see the best in them and expect nothing less than their best. From a very young age, these "elite" kids are given a special advantage that other, oftentimes slightly younger, kids are not.

Over the course of a year, the differences in performance may be small and not that noticeable. But when we project what it means to have better coaching, stronger and more engaged teaching, and additional positive reinforcement over ten years, we realize that we are creating kids who are significantly smarter, who have been trained better, and who have more self-confidence than many of their peers, all because of the early "tryout" they went through when they were very young. This is a result of what sociologist Robert Merton calls the self-fulfilling prophecy, where "a false definition, in the beginning ... evokes a new behavior which makes the original false conception come true."

Children who were selected as gifted at a very young age, often only because of age, become gifted, smarter, stronger, faster, and more talented because they turn the higher expectations placed upon them into reality. As such, your young hockey player is four times more likely to make a travel team if he is born in the first three months of the year, and not the last three months.

I do not say this because I think it is wrong to give elite performers special attention. I say it because as the parent of a young athlete, you need to be cognizant of these facts and how your child fits into the grand scheme of things age- and ability-wise. Is she one of the oldest or youngest in her age group? Does she have success because she is a bit bigger, faster, stronger, and older, or because she works harder than anyone else? Does she struggle because she is smaller, slower, and weaker because of her relative age, and can't be the biggest, fastest, or strongest no matter how hard she tries?

Many great young athletes quit far too soon because they perceive their lack of competence as something that is always within their control, which it is not. There are many others who are not fast-tracked because they happen to be born six or more months after the age cutoff, and their chances for success are therefore diminished. Our system eliminates almost 50 percent of our potential elite performers because of the month they were born. It is crazy!

Game-Changing Questions for Parents

1. What part of the calendar does my child's birthday fall on? Is he or she chronologically advantaged or

disadvantaged? Is it affecting my child's perceived competence?

2. If you are a parent of a "chronologically disadvantaged" child, do not give up hope! Be a parent, because your kids will need you more than many of their peers. They need you to give them the perspective and assurances that one day bigger, faster, and stronger will all even out, and the one who has worked the hardest and played the longest will excel.

In my own coaching experience, I cannot count how many times this happened. I have coached kids who were "not quite there" at age fifteen and playing soccer in the Atlantic Coast Conference (the best college soccer conference in the United States) at age eighteen. I have coached kids who made the club B team at age thirteen and were in the U.S. National Pool for their age group a year later. I have spoken to club directors who told me nearly 75 percent of their A-team athletes at age eleven were no longer on the A team at age eighteen. Early success is not an indicator of later success! The world is filled with late bloomers. They succeed because they have parents, coaches, and teachers who give them perspective and help them realize that their perceived failures are due to factors beyond their control. All they need to do is keep working hard and stay in the game.

I believe it is incredibly important as parents to note whether the system may be putting your children at a disadvantage, and ruining their perceived competence in the process, without you even knowing it. The fact is that kids born more than six months after an arbitrary cutoff can be institutionally and systematically disadvantaged because of the month they were born, not because of their potential to be a great athlete or a brilliant student. They are disadvantaged because six to twelve months of additional mental, physical, and emotional development at prepubescent ages can place kids miles apart in terms of learning, development, and advanced coordination.

Unfortunately, you cannot do much to change the systematic disadvantages for your kids, but you can certainly make sure that you are not contributing to the problem, and exacerbating the situation, by neglecting the factors causing the disadvantage. Find your own slanty line in the classroom or on the field, and make sure your child does not give up before he even had a chance to succeed. You may have a high performer just waiting to blossom.

Overcoming Disappointment

Throughout this book we have emphasized taking the focus off the results and putting it on the process of learning. This is crucial when it comes to failure in sports, because it comes in many forms. One of the most difficult things to deal with as a parent and a coach is tryout time; young athletes' dreams can be crushed if they are not selected. Yet I have found that these times can become the springboard for future success in the presence of great parenting and superb communication.

Most people have heard how Michael Jordan was cut from his high school basketball team, yet he did pretty well for himself. Did you know NBA Hall of Famer John Stockton was not recruited out of high school, or that NFL Hall of Famer Steve Young was the eighth-string quarterback as a freshman at BYU? Young wanted to quit but his dad talked him into sticking it out and fulfilling his commitment. Again, he's got a few Super Bowl rings to remind him that it was worth overcoming a little adversity.

As an adult, every time we deal with a child who has encountered disappointment, we have multiple paths we can take. We are confronted with the choice between making our athlete *feel* better and making our athlete *be* better. I believe we can do both. This is often the path to high performance.

Many parents take the disappointment of getting cut from a team as an opportunity to ridicule the coach, the program, and even the players on the team. They let their emotions get the best of them and try to make their child feel better by criticizing everyone else involved. While this may make the player feel a bit better on the surface, it does nothing to address the reasons for the failure, or make that child a better person because of the disappointment. It often only serves to make the adult feel better, to justify to himself that this coach and team was not worthy of his child's participation. Parents who do this never ask themselves "Who are my actions actually serving?"

A second approach is one that makes the child *be* better. Have a great conversation with your child, be present, listen to and understand what she is feeling, cry with her, and then be the adult. Provide some perspective. Help her understand why this happened and how to prepare differently next time. Great parents do this, and great coaches will take the time to do this for the players they had to cut. It is uncomfortable. It can be awkward and very emotional, but it comes with the territory of being a role model for children.

Once the initial strong emotions of the disappointment have passed, but while the sting is still fresh in their minds, let children try to explain what they are feeling. Then help them shape some new goals that will lead them on the path to success. Make them specific, make them attainable, make them timely, and write them down. A year from now, come tryout time, you may have an athlete with a chip on her shoulder, motivated, brave, and with something to prove. Every coach is looking for those types of kids!

I have faced this situation more than a few times in two decades of coaching, and I loved leaving that initial post-tryout meeting when the kid shook my hand, looked me in the eye, and said, "Coach, I am going to prove you wrong." Throughout the year, I would check in once in a while to let the athlete know I was watching him and keeping tabs. At tryouts a year later, when that athlete left no doubt about who was making that team, well, those are among my proudest moments as a coach. There were times when I looked in a player's eye and nodded my head yes even though he already knew the answer. Those were special moments. These were magic times when I could see the joy and sense of accomplishment swell through a player as he thought about all he had committed to the past year in order to make the team and overcome his disappointment. Times like these were the reason I coached, and the reason I still coach. Those were not just sport accomplishments. They were life achievements.

Game-Changing Questions for Parents

1. Do I help my child overcome disappointment?
2. Have I ever shared with my child times in my life when I have been disappointed and told him/her how I dealt with it?

If you want a high performer, then make your disappointed athlete feel better by making him be better. It is not immediate, it is not easy, but it is perhaps the most valuable gift you can ever give a child.

Action Steps for Gaining Competence

1. Employ the slanty line theory to activities and games to encourage children to compete against their best, and not others.
2. Determine whether your child is one of the oldest or youngest on his team or in his class.
3. If relative age is a factor, help your child understand that he may be temporarily advantaged or disadvantaged, but that does not affect his need to work hard, be committed, and develop skill.
4. If your child is an early bloomer, reinforce the importance of working hard and developing skill, and point out that size and speed advantages will not always exist.

5. Make sure your child's perceived competence is not solely competition-based. Focus on individual improvement and factors that are within his or her control, such as effort, commitment, and focus.
6. Help your child overcome disappointment by not only making him feel better, but be better!

Game-Changing Questions for Your Child

1. What is your role on the team?
2. Do you understand why those kids are bigger, faster, and stronger than you ... or do you know why you are bigger, faster, and stronger than your teammates?
3. Do you understand that eventually everyone will be essentially the same size, speed, etc., and that what matters then is how hard you work and how skilled you are?
4. How can I help you get better?

10

Confidence

Confidence is going after Moby Dick in a rowboat and taking the tartar sauce with you.

—**Zig Ziglar**

Confidence—or the lack thereof—is probably the number-one issue that affects athletic performance and development. Every athlete, even a top professional, has times of diminished performance due to a lack of belief, and other times when it all clicks and he is in the "zone" of high performance. No story better illustrates this than that of major league baseball player Rick Ankiel.

Ankiel was a promising rookie in 2000, winning eleven games for the St. Louis Cardinals, striking out 194 batters and finishing second in the National League Rookie of the Year balloting. Due to injuries to other pitchers, he was selected to start game one of the National League Division Series against the Atlanta Braves, and it all fell apart. After not allowing a run in the first two innings, in the third Ankiel allowed four runs, walked four batters, and threw five wild pitches before being removed.

In his next start in game two of the National League Championship Series against the New York Mets, he was removed after throwing only twenty pitches, five of which flew past catcher Eli Marrero. A four-batter relief appearance in game five of the series yielded two more walks and two more wild pitches.

In 2001, Ankiel began the season with the Cardinals but was soon demoted to Triple A, where in 4.1 innings he walked 17 batters, threw 12 wild pitches, and had an ERA of 20.77! How can a promising young pitcher, who was the second best rookie in 2000 and had thrown thousands of pitches in his life, fall so far and so fast? Rick Ankiel lost his confidence to throw strikes.

Although Ankiel persisted and reinvented himself as a major league outfielder, his struggles were heartbreaking to watch. While his breakdown happened in front of millions of people, it can be even more painful to watch our children go through similar times. We feel helpless and are driven to intervene, which is often the worst thing we can do. Don't lose hope. Once you understand how athletes develop and maintain confidence, the next time your child falls down, you will know what it takes to get him to pick himself back up.

One of the greatest lessons that sports gives our children is the ability to believe in themselves and be confident no matter what obstacles they face or what challenges lie ahead. Confidence derived from sports carries many people through their entire lives. They learn to view challenges as opportunities instead of obstacles to fear. Athletic confidence helps children create a positive mindset throughout life. Confidence is a requirement of consistent high performance. In order to explore the concept further, we will:

1. Define athletic confidence
2. Learn where confidence comes from

3. Discover how kids need to learn from failure and not fear it

4. Explore how and when to praise our children

The Definition of Athletic Confidence

Confidence is a state of mind, a feeling inside that you are ready to perform, no matter what you encounter. It is a feeling of certainty and control that provides an athlete with a positive outlook regardless of the situation. It cannot be bought, it cannot be faked, and it cannot be wished for. Confidence is earned, refined, and developed through the acquisition of skill and the support of confidence-building mentors.

As your child develops competence in a sport, his confidence also increases. Let me say that another way: confidence is a natural byproduct of skill. From a small child to the world's greatest athletes, those who are confident are confident because they have taken thousands of shots, tried and failed many times, then tried again and got it right. Come game time, they believe that the skills they have developed will carry them through. This belief is always at the forefront of their thoughts, instead of the fear of failure that many non-confident athletes possess. Whatever happens, self-doubt rarely enters their thoughts; if it does, their belief in themselves drowns it out.

True athletic confidence is all about the process and the preparation and has little to do with the outcomes of games or events. Confident athletes see wins and losses as inevitable parts of the process, and their self-belief does not waver based upon results. Whether they win or lose, they examine the process that got them the result and recognize areas for improvement rather than find excuses for failure. In the end, the true confidence of high performers is consistent, controllable, and long-lasting.

Where Does Confidence Come From?

Confidence in young athletes is a byproduct of two things: proper preparation and adults who believe in them. Quality training, mental and physical preparation, and even previous success do not ensure confidence. Young athletes also need connection.

It is very important that the adults in your child's life are confidence builders, and it is best when they come from both within and outside of your immediate family. They must model the discipline, hard work, and self-belief that you hope to see in your athlete. They must control their emotions and choose their words wisely and truly understand the specific needs of the athlete. They must also be trustworthy.

Many times in my coaching career I worked with younger coaches who ranted and raved all game long and grew increasingly frustrated as their players quit performing up to their potential. They micromanaged every play, huffed and puffed at every mistake, and yelled and screamed at the players before, during, and after the game. As we dissected the game afterwards, I would often hear the coach say, "I don't know what happened. We worked on that all week. I thought we were prepared." What happened was that the coach did not demonstrate to his players that he believed they were prepared. His words and actions demonstrated something entirely different. Players cannot trust themselves to perform well unless they are trusted by others to do the same.

One of the most important factors in determining confidence is the amount of control an athlete is given. If you want your young athlete to be confident, then do not do things for him that he can do himself. Give him the responsibility for his own actions and decisions. Encourage him to take risks, and allow him to fail. Do not make excuses or blame others; instead just let them go. Young athletes who are able to work out their own problems, and see in their adult mentors the belief and trust to take control, will learn to stand tall and confidently in the face of great adversity.

Confidence building is a long, drawn-out process, and ultimately the process must be owned by the athlete. We can help our children to become confident, but eventually they need to believe in themselves and be responsible for their beliefs. Unfortunately, many parents believe that confidence only comes through success and positive outcomes. They do not realize that the actual process of achieving skill is what creates confidence.

Think about it this way. Is your child more likely to believe she can sink the game-winning free throw if she has made a thousand free throws in practice, or if you have told her a thousand times what a good free-throw shooter she is? Clearly, it is the former. Confidence is a natural byproduct of skill.

Some adults shelter their children from failure and shower them with praise when they succeed. The sad results of this kind of thinking are kids who never become confident athletes. They focus on outcomes rather than process, and they depend upon the adults to instill confident thoughts and behaviors. They cede control and personal responsibility. Building confidence is a process marked by highs and lows, successes and failures. If you always try to protect your child from disappointment, create excuses for failure, or expect self-belief to happen overnight, your athlete might get a lot of things, but confidence will not be one of them.

Game-Changing Question for Parents

Does my child have a confidence-building adult in our family? Does he have a coach, teacher, or other adult outside our immediate family that helps him build confidence?

Allow Them to Fail

To try is to risk failure. But risks need to be taken, because the greatest hazard in life is to risk nothing. The person who risks nothing, does nothing, has nothing and is nothing. They may avoid suffering and sorrow, but they cannot learn, feel change, grow, love and live. Chained by their certitudes, they are a slave; they have forfeited their freedom. Only a person who risks is free.

—Leo Buscaglia

One of the most valuable lessons your child will learn from sports is how to take risks, how to fail gracefully, and ultimately how to succeed by overcoming failure. Sport is a microcosm of life, and life is a series of challenges and disappointments, where many times you must pick yourself up, dust yourself off, and get on with it. Take a close look at the successful people you know. They have all failed. In fact, *the most successful people are often the ones who have failed most often.*

It has been said, "What would you dream to do if you knew that you could not fail?" Unfortunately the fear of failure is pervasive in our children and can eventually lead to low self-confidence, lack of motivation, depression, anxiety, and more

Studies show that the fear of failure is usually caused by parents and develops when children are under the age of ten. These children are so scarred by their fear of failing and disappointing their parents that they avoid any activities, sports, and educational challenges that may not end in success. It will be difficult for them to become high performers because they will be afraid to risk achievement in the first place. Remember Carol Dweck's studies on fixed-mindset individuals? Children with a fixed mindset judge themselves completely upon achievement and thus will never risk anything that does not guarantee success.

It's okay for our kids to fail, and they must not fear failure. It is our job as parents to make sure that our children are not afraid to strike out, to miss an open goal, to slice it into the woods, and to lose "important" games. It is our job to instill a growth mindset in our young athletes. They need such a mindset because they will fail many times in their life, and they need to learn from failure instead of fearing it. Youth sports should be the safest place for them to experience failure for the first time.

Sport allows them to face challenges and overcome adversity in a place and time where it matters in a small sense but does not matter in the big picture. It should be safe because these challenges and failures should not have the same consequences as failure at a job, failure in a relationship, and failure as a parent may have. They will learn incredibly valuable lessons in overcoming challenges, so when the stakes are much bigger, they face them with confidence and clarity of purpose.

High performers also need to learn that they can succeed without your intervention, because you will not always be there for them. Through youth sports, they can learn that even if they fail you are proud of them for trying and love them unconditionally. As a result, instead of fearing failure, high performers learn to embrace and overcome challenges. They learn that you have their back, unconditionally, always. If there is a better venue to learn this than youth sports, I have not seen it.

Game-Changing Question for Parents

What is your child's attitude toward failure? Does she see failure as part of the learning process or something to be avoided? Ask yourself, "Have I been forthcoming with my child about the times in my life when I failed, and how I overcame failure?"

Messy Is Good!

Youth sports is like feeding a two-year-old oatmeal; it's going to be really messy at first, with a lot of failure and very little success, but ultimately your child will learn to give herself nourishment. As a parent, you sometimes feel compelled to intervene on behalf of your frustrated (and hungry) child, and there are certainly times when you can and should step in. But you also have to recognize that as long as you keep feeding your child, she will never learn to eat on her own. Sports activities are the same way, regardless of whether your child is five and playing a sport for the first time or getting ready to head off to college.

Many parents feel compelled to protect their young children from all adversity and failure. The need to protect our children is one of the strongest emotions we ever feel, and one of the hardest to ignore, yet deep down we know that eventually we have to allow our children, even compel them, to figure it out on their own.

Our job is to try to strike a balance between success and failure. Too much of either is harmful. Many young prodigies fizzle out as they encounter challenges at an older age, for they never learned how to fail when they were young. Their early success made them complacent, and they never learned to work hard and challenge themselves. Others who are protected by their parents from ever failing are unprepared when real obstacles and competition are present and their overprotective parents are not.

By the same token, a child who is put in an achievement activity and only experiences failure will become disillusioned, lose confidence, and eventually avoid the activity. Our goal is to strike a balance. When we do, as Dr. Jim Taylor says, "Success is not such an intoxicant that it inhibits further growth, and failure is not such a monumental loss that it diminishes the desire to pursue success. Rather, they are both inevitable and necessary parts of the process leading toward achievement and happiness."

Think about your own life and what you learned whenever you failed at work, in sports, or in a relationship. You learned how to overcome disappointment, as well as how to be creative and work through problems. You learned how to tolerate and minimize frustration and eventually to ask for assistance if needed. These are incredibly valuable life lessons about which you probably look back upon and say "I'm glad that happened; I learned so much from that."

Try to recall how good you always felt when you overcame adversity, when you solved a difficult problem and found success where others failed. This is among our most powerful emotions, the feeling of achievement after challenging ourselves. It charges our spirit, gives us belief, and puts a big smile on our face and in our soul. Imagine if you never got the chance to feel this way. You wouldn't ever know what it feels like to live! Why take this away from your kids?

Your children will never learn to overcome the big disappointments in life if they are not allowed to overcome the small ones that sports activities bring to them. I know there is a great fear among parents that failure, no matter how small and inconsequential, is devastating for kids' self-esteem, but research demonstrates that this is not true. Bad experiences are not destructive to your child's self-esteem; in fact, quite the opposite is true. Self-esteem comes from achievement and not the other way around. So let them fail while daring greatly, and in the end they will find success and the great sense of accomplishment that comes along with it.

How to Praise Your Child

Parents often ask me, "How do I praise my child, and when is it too much or too little?" Many parents fear that if they do not excessively praise their children, their kids will feel unloved and uncared for. The result is over-praise, and their kids see right through it. I have seen many athletes tell their mom and dad, "You're just saying that because you are my parents," and they are right. Learning how to praise appropriately, and what to praise, is an important part of developing a child's confidence and raising a high performer.

Praise Effort

In *The Talent Code*, Dan Coyle explores where greatness comes from by analyzing various centers of excellence, from Brazilian soccer to Russian tennis, from music to education. It is an exploration of the best practices for nurturing and growing talented high achievers. Coyle also cited the work of Stanford University psychologist Dr. Carol Dweck, specifically her studies on the relationship between motivation and language, and her analysis of the effect of verbal cues on response and performance. In one of her most fascinating studies, Dweck tested the effect of a single sentence of praise on the performance of four hundred New York fifth and sixth graders.

Dweck tested the children by giving them some simple puzzles to solve and then met with each of them afterwards to give them the results and a single sentence of praise. Half the children were praised for their intelligence ("You must be smart at this") and the other half for their effort ("You must have worked really hard").

The kids were given a second test and had a choice between taking a harder test or an easier one. Ninety percent of the kids who were praised for their effort chose the hard test, while a majority of the kids praised for their intelligence chose the easier one. "When we praise kids for their intelligence," wrote Dweck, "we tell them that's the name of the game: look smart, don't risk making mistakes."

Dweck then administered a third test, much harder than the previous two, and none of the participants scored particularly well. She was most surprised by their responses to the hard test. The group praised for effort "dug in and grew very involved with the test, trying solutions, testing strategies. They later said they liked it," she reported. "But the group praised for its intelligence hated the harder test. They took it as proof they weren't smart."

Finally, Dweck administered a fourth test, similar in difficulty to the initial one. The results were shocking. The praised-for-effort group improved their initial score by 30 percent, while the praised-for-intelligence kids' scores declined by 20 percent, all because of six words of praise. She was so surprised that she reran the study five different times, and each one had the same results. "We are exquisitely attuned to messages telling us what is valued," says Dweck. "When a clear message comes, it can send a spark."

Dan Coyle found a common denominator among the talent hotbeds that he studied; they all used a type of motivational messaging based upon effort and not outcomes. Brazilian soccer teams call their youth teams the "Aspirantes," the Hopeful Ones. At the Spartak Tennis Academy in Moscow, the home of many of the top players in the world, they don't "play" tennis; they prefer the word *borot'sya*, meaning to struggle or fight. Talent hotbeds and the coaches that run them ignite passion in their children by focusing their praise on the process and emphasizing that learning is a struggle, that it is hard, and that it is not immediately gratifying.

Praising effort works because it gives credence to the baby steps, the difficulty, and the determination that constitutes the learning process. It gives credence to both failure and success. Focusing on the effort instead of the outcome keeps coaches and parents present with our children in their struggle, holding their hand and even carrying them at times. It makes us a partner in the process and allows our athletes to give their attention to the journey and not the destination. It also allows parents and coaches to recognize everything our young athletes are accomplishing along that journey. Praising effort prevents us from being so focused on the prize that we forget to give credence to what got our athlete there. High performers are all about the process, and the process is all about effort.

Be Clear and Concise

Dr. Carol Dweck's research shows us that the clarity of the message, rather than the quantity of messages, has the greatest influence upon performance. It is therefore incredibly important that we understand not only how to praise but when to praise so that our message and our love come across crystal clear to our young athletes.

Your praise should come in the form of encouragement for your child and should be specific, clear, and focused on the process. "Good job today" is nice, but it's not action-, effort-, or goal-specific. On the other hand, "You've really been training hard, and today you put it all together in that race. You could not have done that last year" encourages your child for their effort, their perseverance, their progress, and their competence. It gives them ownership and control over the result and demonstrates that you have been paying attention to their effort throughout the year. It activates your child on multiple levels and sets the stage for further improvement, additional goal setting, and continued improvement.

Try not to over-praise your child. We all know parents who are afraid that their child's self-esteem will suffer if they are not encouraged and praised for every outcome, and this is not true. Over-praising your child can be a negative on two fronts. First, children can become apathetic to praise, since they hear it all the time. You will run out of superlatives and be unable to discern real achievement from the everyday norm. Second, kids are smart, and they soon catch on if everything they do is "fantastic" or "brilliant" or "awesome." It's not, and your kids eventually know a good performance from a bad one. They will grow cynical to your words if everything is incredible.

Do not attempt to praise your child by comparing them to others. There are better ways to encourage your child than to constantly remind them "you are the best player on your team." Maybe they are, and if so they probably know it already. They don't need you to put down their teammates or opponents. This is also not process-specific because in the grand scheme of things the process is all about things you can control, and teammates and opponents do not fit that category. Being the best player on a team of average performers does not say much, while being the twelfth man on the 1992 Olympic Basketball Dream Team was quite an accomplishment for Christian Laettner, don't you think?

Finally, be very careful about sarcastic praise, such as "You really tore it up out there today" after your son goes 3 for 20 from the field in a basketball game. Some players respond to sarcastic comments made at opportune times, but such comments are not appropriate before, during, or after an event or game. All sarcasm has a hint of truth, and kids are so emotional that it is very difficult to know if it will go over well with a young athlete. While I have seen some coaches get away with it, I cannot think of a single instance where sarcasm came across well from a parent to their child. It is best to find other ways to encourage and motivate your athletes.

Game-Changing Question for Parents
When I praise my child, do I praise effort or outcomes?

Gaining confidence is one of the most important lessons youth sports can teach our children and a crucial component of high performance. Our kids need our help to recognize that confidence is a result of preparation. They need to know we believe in them and that they have coaches, teachers, or other mentors who believe in them as well. Once these things are in place, give them control and responsibility. Praise them for their hard work, allow them to fail, and through failure help them to be brave and overcome adversity. Make sure they not only feel better, but be better. That is parenting and coaching at the master level. That is how confidence grows. And that is how high performers are made. As inspirational author Mary Anne Radmacher says:

> Courage doesn't always roar. Sometimes courage is the quiet voice at the end of the day saying, "I will try again tomorrow."[24]

Action Steps for Developing Confidence in Young Athletes
1. Take a good hard look at your child in training and competition, and ask yourself "Does my child display confidence, or is he/she scared?"
2. Look for opportunities to give your child more control over the athletic process. This displays your trust, which helps to grow confidence.

3. Do not always intervene when your child is failing. Allow it to happen, and then discuss the reasons for the outcome (i.e., lack of preparation, lack of focus, etc.).

4. Keep your attention, and that of your child, on the process, on the controllable things, and look for ways to measure improvement.

5. Praise effort.

6. Try not to over-praise or praise sarcastically.

7. Do not compare your child to others; keep the focus on the process.

8. Love them and display that love no matter what.

Game-Changing Questions for Your Child

1. Do you feel confident? Do you know where confidence comes from?

2. How can I help you be more confident?

3. Discuss a recent time when your child has not been successful, and help them understand the reasons why.

4. How do you feel when I praise you? Criticize you?

5. What can I do differently to help your confidence?

11

Caring

Never doubt that a small group of thoughtful, committed citizens can change the world. Indeed, it is the only thing that ever has.

—**Margaret Mead**, cultural anthropologist

Who is your child's favorite spectator? Sorry, but for most kids it is not you, mom and dad. Nor is it their sister or brother, boyfriend or girlfriend. It is grandma and grandpa. Why? Because they love their grandchildren unconditionally, no matter what the score.

I remember playing in a middle school baseball game with both my parents and grandparents in attendance. I think I went 0-4 with three strikeouts, and after the game I was very depressed. As I slunk over to my grandparents, my grandmother yelled, "John, you did wonderful today!"

"But Grandma," I said. "I struck out three times!"

"Yes, but you swung so hard! We are so proud of you." Then we went and got ice cream. A young boy was smiling again, all because of the unconditional love of grandma and grandpa.

We all love our kids, but sometimes we love them in less than helpful ways. I'm often asked, "How can I show my child that I love him, but at the same time push him to get better?" The good news is you can do this by creating some simple boundaries and by being keenly aware of your words and actions before, during, and after your child's athletic events. To do so, we must:

1. Never use love as a weapon to control our kids
2. Be our child's #1 fan, and understand that at her games we can only be a coach, a referee, or a fan, and never all three

Love Is Not a Weapon

Children need to feel cared for and to know with certainty that they are loved regardless of the outcome of any game or match. Take a second and think about your actions and reactions after your child's last sporting event. Did you smile and say "I love watching you play?" Or did you storm off to the car because your daughter's team gave up a last-minute goal? Maybe your child did not play a lot, or their team "was not into it." If you reacted negatively, you have just told your daughter that your love is tied to her performance, and that is a very slippery slope. I have actually given kids a ride home after they were left at the field by a parent who was angry at a result!

It is very dangerous when parents use their love as a reward for performance and withhold their love when the results are not what they want. Wielding love as a weapon to control your children, and basing love upon success and failure, forces your children to focus on outcomes and not the learning process. Many parents do this inadvertently and demonstrate happiness or disappointment through their body language and demeanor. Children feed off this parental emotion and learn that the only way to elicit a happy response—your love—is to succeed on the field or in the classroom. They lose sight of the journey and the things they have control over. It can be quite damaging emotionally to your child and have lasting consequences.[25]

Be Your Child's #1 Fan

One of the best ways to demonstrate your unconditional caring and love for your child is to simply be her #1 fan when you attend her games and practices. Don't be her coach (unless you are actually the coach), don't be the official, just be a fan. Knowing your role and embracing your role is crucial to establishing the unconditional love that your child needs to see in you.

The most important role we play in our children's lives is that of parent. We are not their best friend; they have plenty of peers for that role. We can have an open, trusting, and loving relationship with our kids, but our children need us to be a parent above all else.

A parent/child relationship is not one of equality. It scares me when parents tell me that they are their child's best friends. It makes me wonder why the child does not have any best friends her own age, and why the parents do not either. Parenting is not a relationship between equals, and children need boundaries, authority, and people who are not afraid to say no, to push them, or to make them do things they would not do on their own in their pursuit of achievement in sports, education, or any other type of activity. Kids have plenty of opportunities to find friends but very few to find parents. Embrace this role and do it well. Your friendship with your child will eventually develop out of mutual trust and respect.

You cannot be both a parent and your child's best friend. In a parent/child relationship, there is a clear delineation of decision making and authority. A friendship, on the other hand, denotes a relationship between equals, which you and your child are not when it comes to important decision making. Being your child's best friend does not allow you to push them or lead them or make tough decisions on their behalf. Furthermore, friends are responsible for each other's happiness, and to place the burden of your happiness upon your son or daughter is not a healthy thing. It is much simpler to just be his or her parent. They may not appreciate it much today, but they will thank you for it later.

As the parent, one of the most important things you can do is recognize and embrace your role when you attend your child's competition. There are only three things you can do while watching your child's competition, and you should only be one of these at a time. They are:

- Be a coach
- Be an official
- Be a fan

Each of these roles seems self-explanatory and comes with its own set of responsibilities, each of which is incredibly important to the growth and development of your child. When you go to your child's game or match, you can be only one of these things, and every time you cross the line and try to do two or more roles, you end up confusing your child.

The Role of a Coach

Are you a coach for your child? Have you been designated by the team, the club, or the school to be the person who teaches the game, runs practices, sets the strategy and tactics, and then executes them on game day? If so, and you are coaching your own child, then you face a specific set of unique circumstances which I will deal with below. But if you are not the team coach, and you have dropped your daughter off at training all week and gone about your business, then do not coach her come game time. It does not help her if you arrive on Saturday and start telling your daughter and her teammates where to run, how to hit, where to pass, or when to shoot.

The reason we only have one teacher in school is so kids do not get confused by conflicting instructions in the classroom. Imagine there were twenty-eight sets of parents there each day during math. Come game day, though, oftentimes the head coach is drowned out by the sixteen parent-coaches yelling conflicting instructions to the players on the field. The result, more often than not, is not action but inaction from the player. She does not know who to listen to, the adult her parents have told her is the coach and should be respected, or mom and dad screaming their lungs out, living and dying on each play and often contradicting the coach's instructions.

I cannot tell you the number of players I coached who were very different players depending upon which side of the field they played: the coach's side or the spectators' side. On one side they were confident, decisive, inventive, and a risk taker, while on the other they became timid and often negative in their play and demeanor. Come game time, players perform best when they have a mindset that allows them both the freedom and the responsibility to learn, to succeed, and especially to fail. If you are unsure, ask your child how he would like you to act and what to say. You might be surprised by the answer.

Coaching Your Own Child

If you happen to be asked to be your child's designated coach, you are often in a difficult and unenviable position of having to balance the needs of your child with the overall needs of his or her team. It happens a lot, as it is estimated that nearly 75-80 percent of youth sports coaches end up coaching their own child. It can also happen on the highest levels, a recent example being U.S. National Men's Soccer Team Coach Bob Bradley, who had his son Michael on the team (starting, playing a significant role, even scoring in the 2010 World Cup). I wish there was a perfect answer here, but I don't think there is one.

Game-Changing Questions for the Parent Coach

Start by answering these three questions for yourself, and if one of your answers raises some red flags, think long and hard about taking on a coaching role for your child:

- What is my relationship with my child, and how will coaching her affect that relationship? Are we already at odds in our relationship, or is it a good one that can withstand this situation?
- What is my relationship with the other children on the team, who may be my child's friends, and how will my coaching affect those relationships? If your child is very close with the kids on the team, you may have to coach them, be critical of them, even discipline them, and it can change the relationship between your child and her friends, which can ultimately change your relationship with your child.
- How will my coaching affect my relationships with the parents of my child's teammates?

If you can comfortably answer these questions for yourself, then talk to your child and see what he has to say. If he is fine with it, make sure he understands that when you are home you are dad, and when you are on the field you are the coach. The Positive Coaching Alliance recommends that you explain to your child, "I always love you and you are special to me. But when I'm coaching you, I need to treat you like all the other players. And you need to respond to me as your coach, not your dad. Do you think you can do that?"[26]

Make sure you are being fair to your child and to his teammates. It is extremely important to be cognizant of, and deal with, other parents' and players' perceptions. Are you playing favorites, letting your child play more minutes or more coveted positions? The best way to combat this is to lay out the team goals and expectations to the team parents and players before the season, and then consistently follow through with them. Getting everyone on the same page, and sticking to that page, resolves a lot of issues.

Many times I worked with mom and dad coaches who held their own kids to higher standards than everyone else in order to be "fair." This can be equally damaging to a child who never gets to be "just a player" and be himself once in a while. Usually everyone recognized this except the parent, and it was often my job to get him to see the effect on his child. The best coaches I worked with knew when to say enough and pass the torch of coaching that team to another coach so they could go back to being a parent.

Be sure to take your coaching hat off when you leave the field. Do not discuss sensitive team information with, or in front of, your child unless it pertains directly to them. It is best to leave the coaching to practice time and just be a parent the rest of the time. If you do not, your child will never get a break from practice, and it will strain your relationship.

Finally, and perhaps counter-intuitively, whenever you can, don't coach your own kid! This may sound silly, but part of releasing your child to the game is not being there every practice and game, and micromanaging another part of your child's life. When your kids are young, even if you have expertise in a certain sport and get along great with your kids when you coach them, it is probably best if you are not the head coach season after season. Offer to help out, to run a practice or two, but remember that you can say I love you to your daughter just as easily by not coaching her as by coaching her. Ask your child if they want you to coach, explain to them why you will not coach them all the time, and give them the opportunity to say "Thanks, Dad, but I want Billy's dad to coach basketball for us." Kids cannot be themselves when mom or dad is always the coach, or when play time is always at their house, so once in a while you need to let them go and coach less.

The Role of Official

I can think of no more thankless job in the United States than that of youth sports official. From baseball to soccer, hockey to basketball, officials are held to levels of perfection and proficiency far higher than we hold ourselves to in our day-to-day lives. When they don a striped jersey on Saturday they become public enemy number one. This is wrong.

Across the United States, in all sports, it is becoming more difficult to recruit, train, and retain youth sports officials, as many of them tire quickly from the relentless badgering by parents, players, and coaches. Season after season, referee associations in numerous sports are replacing up to 70 percent of their new officials, as burnout, low pay, and dissatisfaction among many officials lead them to move on to greener pastures. What was once a fun hobby has been spoiled by misguided coaches and parents who treat officials as though every game is the World Cup final or game seven of the NBA playoffs.

When you go to watch your child's sporting event, you must remember that you are going there as a fan and not to officiate. When you live and die with every call, when you scream in disagreement at an official decision, you not only make the environment a negative learning one for your child, but you set an incredibly poor example for him. I cannot count how many times I have heard parents castigate their kids for receiving a yellow card in soccer for talking back to officials, while at the same time they berated that official for ninety minutes from the opposite sideline. We cannot expect young children to respect the officials if they spend the entire game listening to their parents disrespect them.

I believe this points to an even larger problem, namely the declining lack of respect for adults and authority figures in our society. We have officials, referees, and judges in sports to be the ultimate adjudicators in all disputes, yet we turn on the TV and players are in the official's face on each and every call (especially in professional baseball and soccer, where it is appalling at times). We do not allow our kids to yell at their teachers in school, talk back to the school principal, or question each and every decision we make for them as parents. But for some reason in youth sports it has become acceptable, and I believe that disrespect has begun to leach into schools, into homes, and into everyday life. This is not a healthy trend by any means, and perhaps we should start the pendulum swinging in the opposite direction by setting a better example in sports. That starts with all of us adults on the sideline.

Special Note Regarding Young Officials and Referees

One very alarming trend I see, and quite a disgusting one at that, is the adults who do not reserve their referee abuse for fellow adults but dish it out equally to youth officials as well. I have seen parents at an eleven-year-old soccer game going ballistic, screaming and intimidating a center or an assistant referee over a missed offside call, a missed foul, or, gasp, getting a call wrong on a throw-in. Oftentimes this assistant referee is the same age as the players they are refereeing!

A parent would never scream like that at their own kid for hitting a bad pass or running to the wrong place on the field, but he has no problem screaming at and intimidating an eleven-year-old referee for making a similar technical or judgment error! I know many parents of young referees who must attend games and protect their child from verbal abuse and intimidation. Would you let your son work at an ice cream parlor if you had to go to work with him every day to protect him from irate customers? I think this is crazy.

The fact is we need young referees to replenish the pool each year. These young referees need to cut their teeth in recreational and youth games in settings where the result does not really matter. They have to learn in games for our youngest players before taking the next steps and advancing in the certification process. Many of them never get beyond their first season, as making a few bucks is just not worth the abuse they take. There is no other situation these kids have to face outside of sports where they take such abuse from adults. It does not happen in school, not in their social time, and hopefully not in their own homes. But look out if you want to referee.

All of us have probably stood by at one time and allowed this abuse to happen. We would never let someone berate our own child like this, and certainly would not stand by and allow such bullying on a playground or in another public place. For some reason, because it's a game and someone signed up to be a referee, all bets are off. "They signed up to be a referee, they knew what they were getting into" is a refrain I have heard from some parents when told by an event official to stop. No, it's not what they signed up for, it is not acceptable. Do not be a bystander; it is our responsibility to put a stop to this type of behavior and stand up to abusive adults.

Be a Fan!

What does it mean to be a fan? Well, as we have discussed above, it means that you are not a player, you are not there to coach, and you are definitely not there to referee. You are there to cheer, to support, and to encourage. You are there to show through your presence, your actions, and your emotions that you are proud of your kids. You are there to demonstrate that this is only a game and not a life-or-death situation that will influence your love for your son or daughter. That is what being a fan is all about. Nothing more and nothing less.

Game-Changing Questions for Parents

1. What role do I play at my child's athletic events?
2. Do I try to play more than one?

The Responsibilities of a Sports Parent

Being a fan starts well before the first kick of the game, for if you have not noticed, your child's performance improves when they receive praise and positive reinforcement. The Positive Coaching Alliance (PCA) calls this filling your child's emotional tank, or e-tank. When the tank is full, your child can perform better and longer. They are more coachable and open to suggestion, and are not as easily discouraged when faced with adversity. Conversely, a child with an empty e-tank can get defensive and easily discouraged. The secret is how to fill up the tank.

The PCA suggests the following methods:

- Be a good listener: encourage your child to tell you more about what they are learning and what they like about their sports.
- Be truthful and specific with praise: instead of saying "Great job," say, "It was great when you picked your head up and made that awesome pass to Tim for the goal." Specific praise shows that you are watching their game carefully and you care.
- Your actions and reactions, such as a thumbs-up, a wink, or a smile, mean the world to your kids and can really fill the e-tank.

Just as the above methods can fill the tank, doing the opposite can be a tank drainer. If you don't listen to them, or ignore them, it drains them. If you fail to pay attention and are on your phone when they score the big goal and look your way, or if you are sarcastic and demeaning, it can really drain their tank and negatively affect their performance. Try to keep your hands off your hips, your arms uncrossed, and your phone in your pocket. Be present and engaged during your child's events and you will fill that e-tank!

The Pre-Game Car Ride

Many a big game has been lost, and many a performance has been ruined, before a single player even steps on the field. It's called the car ride to the game! As a coach I waged many a battle against the "statistics dad." He was the guy who told the vanload of kids on the way to the game how their upcoming opponent scored 62 goals and only gave up 3, had not lost in two years, and how their smallest player was bigger than him and had already committed to Stanford at age twelve! Stats Dad soon realized that the kids in the van were no longer smiling but scared to death, so he closed with "Oh, but you guys will be fine, you can win." And then he handed them off to me with a quick "Go get 'em, coach, these girls are ready!" Ready to what, puke?

Your kids take cues from you, plain and simple, and when you make it clear that this moment is so huge, so important, and so impossible a task, how do you think a twelve-year-old is going to react? Do you work well if you are told that if you mess up you are fired? Could you complete a task at work if you knew that your coworkers and boss were going to yell at you constantly and micromanage your work? If you have to talk before or during the game, then fill kids' tanks with belief, with confidence, and talk them through ways they can be successful. Better yet, just leave them alone and let them figure it out. They might just surprise you.

Game-Changing Question for Parents

What kind of cues am I sending to my kids before and during games? Am I modeling confidence in their abilities or something else?

Your kids hear what you say, but they are more likely to believe what they see. While being a fan and being a coach are quite different in many regards, one aspect where they are the same is in how players perceive your reactions to certain events during competition. Next time you are at a youth sporting event, take a look at what players do after a big mistake, a strikeout, or a missed scoring opportunity. They often put their head down, then look at their coach, and then look for their parents. They are looking to see how mom and dad reacted to their error. If mom and dad are sitting there, holding their heads in shame, faces buried in their hands, they are visually telling their child that what he has done is not good. They are reinforcing all the negative thoughts that are going through his own head in that moment. They are telling him that it is okay to dwell on his mistake because that is exactly what they are doing. Ultimately, and most damaging, they are telling him that his value is tied to athletic performance. It is sad to hear many young athletes talk about "that look on my mom's face when I didn't do well."

What if your daughter turned to you during the game and saw you clapping and mouthing "great effort" to her as she jogged by. What if she saw you smile, or wink, or give a thumbs-up, telling her it's okay, to get on with it, to play the next play and forget about the last one. What if she saw you laughing and giggling before the big game instead of looking like you were shipping her off to war? This simple little switch in your actions and reactions can play a huge role in your child's love of the game and an even bigger role in her ability to perform in competition.

Coaches know there is no way to know if a player can make the game-winning shot, or perform in the close game, unless they give her that chance. As a parent, I am often amazed at what my kids can accomplish if I just give them the opportunity to figure it out. It is crucially important that we convey this to our kids through our actions and reactions. In my coaching I have always adhered to the famous Henry Ford quote: "Whether you think you can or think you can't, you're right." Let's make sure that when our kids look at us, they know that we believe in them, and that we think they can succeed!

The Parental Code of Conduct . . .
Written by Your Kids

Here is a novel idea. While we are very fond of handing our players rules, regulations, and codes of conduct, we rarely hand them to our parents. When we do, the usual reaction is for them to bristle at the suggestion that the club they are paying good money to is telling them how to act, how to cheer, and how to properly support their kids.

Parents are correct to a point. It does not make a lot of sense to hand them a bunch of rules written in some boardroom and never explain to them why this is important. Rules are just arbitrary dictums that are always tested, protested, and eventually broken. Rules govern by fear and threat, not by a voluntary change in behavior and attitude.

Instead, we need standards. Standards are not fixed. Standards are commonly held beliefs that are to be aspired to instead of adhered to. Teams, clubs, and schools with high standards do not need excessive rules, for people act correctly because they know it is beneficial for their kids, and not because they are required to do it. Standards allow for discretion by coaches, clubs, and administrators.

That being said, let's have the players decide upon the standards they want their parents to aspire toward. Let's allow the players to write the Parental Code of Conduct. I believe our player-generated Code of Conduct for their parents would look something like this:

I, Johnny's dad, promise to do the following:

- Cheer for everyone on the team, not just certain players, and not just my child
- Cheer for the team, but not too much
- Cheer and encourage the team at appropriate times and in a civilized manner
- Support the team win or lose
- Support my child even when he is not playing much
- Praise my child when he does something right
- Leave him alone on the ride home after games
- Tell him "I enjoy watching you play" after every game and really mean it
- Just be there for my child, and share his sports goals instead of imposing mine

- Provide him with the appropriate push when his actions are not matching his own goals
- Remind him to keep working hard no matter what
- Remember that my child chooses to play for fun and is trying his best
- Don't be too hard on my child, allow him to fail, and be patient
- Give him some room to grow, but stay by his side to help him grow up
- Keep everything in perspective
- Model good behavior
- Help make sports fun
- Be the sports parent I wish I had

I, Johnny's dad, promise not to do the following, because it makes my son feel embarrassed or uncomfortable:

- Yell or scream at the referees, players, or coaches
- Try to coach the coach
- Make discouraging comments to players or about players
- Yell at my son when he is trying to concentrate, because it makes him play worse
- Criticize other athletes or coaches, before, during, or after games
- Cheer if the other team makes a mistake
- Boo at bad calls or opponents' success
- Tell my son what he needs to do better when I know less about the game than he does
- Try to improve my son's game with my negativity. I will let him enjoy himself during the game.
- Act as if I do not love my child after games when we lose
- Make sports over-important at the expense of the rest of our family

If you want a happy young athlete who performs at a high level, then become your child's #1 fan and love him unconditionally, regardless of results. Cheer for him, cheer for his teammates, and do so in a respectful and civilized manner. Be the sports parent you wish you had, and your child's smile and hug after the game will be all the certainty you ever need that you are doing the right thing.

Action Steps for Demonstrating That Your Child Is Unconditionally Loved

- After every event, tell your child "I love watching you play."
- Be aware of your actions and reactions to both positive and negative outcomes. React to process and progress, and remain calm and loving during competition.
- Be your child's number #1 fan
- Fill your child's emotional tank.
- Make sure your actions match your intentions, and your reactions do as well.
- Follow the Parental Code of Conduct … Written by Your Kids

Game-Changing Questions for Your Child

1. How would you like me to act when I come to your games?
2. What do I do that is helpful when I watch you play? What would you like me to do differently?
3. Would you like to write a Code of Conduct for our sideline behavior?

PART III

CHANGING THE YOUTH SPORTS MINDSET

12

The Change
Begins at Home

But one doesn't wait for a revolution. One becomes it.
—**Carl Safina**, *The View from Lazy Point*

I am quite certain that the solution to our youth sports issues in the United States will not come from the top. Our country will not form a national youth sports governing body with the authority to set standards and mandate costs, playing seasons, etc. It goes against our very notions of freedom and capitalism to mandate from a quasi-governmental authority. The change will also not come from the corporations and organizations making money off of youth sports, for they benefit greatly from the status quo. Change will happen if we:

1. Start small and make changes in our family
2. Use our positive changes as an example to change our team
3. Help change ripple out to our community and our country

Start Small

Change can happen, but it will only come from parents like you who do not accept the status quo and insist on change. Bit by bit, school by school, state by state, and sport by sport you can change the game for our kids. Do not be daunted by the immensity of the task, for change can be small and gradual. Change can start with a whisper, with your family, with your team, and grow from there. But you must start at home by raising your own happy and high-performing athlete. As Mother Teresa advised us, "Never worry about numbers. Help one person at a time and always start with the person nearest you."

This book has been full of different suggestions and ideas about how to make sports an incredible experience for your children. By finding them a safe and developmentally appropriate place to play, and communicating well with them, you allow them to gain competence and skill. Their newfound ability breeds confidence, which grows when they realize that your love for them is never tied to wins and losses. And by keeping the big picture in mind, you maintain a healthy vision for the role of sports in your children's lives and in your family. You maintain balance, and regardless of the cost of sports, if your child becomes confident, compassionate, bold, and honest, you might agree that those things are priceless. This is just the beginning.

Remember the last time you bought a new car, read a great book, or tried a fantastic new recipe? What did you do? You told others about it! Not in a judgmental way, as in "The new way my wife cooks chicken is so much better than anything you guys cook. You should try it!" Of course not, because that only offends people and pretty much guarantees that they will not listen.

On the other hand, what if you send them the recipe with a short note that says "I know how much you guys like roast chicken. Check out this new recipe we found; I think you will like it." This does not threaten them or judge their current status; it just suggests there might be another good way, even a better way, to prepare a meal. Well, I think parenting advice is kind of the same thing; approach the subject delicately, non-judgmentally, and do not get in your friend's face about it. They may think they have the greatest recipe in the world for raising children, and who knows, they might. All you are doing is suggesting there might be an alternative one.

Be a pebble in their shoe. Have your suggestion be that little thing that sits in the back of their mind, the thing that comes to their attention every time they take a wrong step or events do not turn out as they hoped. Through your words, and especially your actions, model the behavior you want others to model. Help your own child to get the most out of sports, and always maintain perspective. Eventually other parents will ask "What are you guys doing? How come you are always so happy and never nervous before our games? Why does your daughter always look like she's having fun? Why do all your sports trips seem like vacations?"

"Well, it's funny you should ask. I kind of felt like you did until…" And you are off. The revolution has begun.

We are free to change the world we live in, and that goes for the sports our kids play as well. We all have the freedom to make positive changes, and I would argue that we also have the obligation to as well. We are obligated because whether we like it or not, the families on our child's sports teams are part of our child's sports experience. One bad apple can ruin the whole bunch and make sports less rewarding and certainly less fun not only for a person's own kids but for everyone on the team. Whether he yells at referees, second guesses the coach, coaches the team from the sideline, or just makes his own child so miserable that it affects everyone else, this adult is having a tremendous impact on your child's athletic experience.

This leaves you with a choice: quit the team after the season is over or lead the change for your own child and eventually your own team. Spread the word, and some people will listen right away. As for the others? Well, just be a pebble in their shoe. They will either see the difference in your child and make a change, or they will leave. Either way, problem solved for your team.

I think many of us go through life always wondering if the grass is greener on the other side, especially when it comes to sports. As a young coach, I know I did, always saying to myself "If I only had those players" or "If I only had that facility." Then I realized that the problem was not whether the grass was greener; the issue was that I was not watering my own grass, which could have been just as green. The same goes for youth sports.

Sure, the club next door might offer a bit more (at least in appearances), but why not take care of your own club, why not water your own grass? That is the kind of change that really makes a difference for your children, for it shows them that change is possible and even probable. As John F. Kennedy said, "The one unchangeable certainty is that nothing is certain or unchangeable."

Change Your Club

By taking positive steps to raise your own child to be a high performer, and make sports a more rewarding experience for him, you also change your club or your school. Happiness spreads, and other parents will take note if your child is happy (and likely a high performer as a result). Now you have begun to change your team. Once other teams see what you are doing and the excellence your team is experiencing, they will want to emulate that as well. Now you have begun to change your club.

Most youth sports organizations devote time and resources into coaching education; only the best make a concerted effort to educate the parents as well. In reality, we parents are also coaches many hours a day to our kids (just not at the game please!). In fact, we coach our kids far more than their actual coaches do. Yet many organizations neglect this crucial aspect of player development. They relegate parents to the sideline and tell us "Step aside, please, this is my show." This may work once in a while, but only when parents are forced to comply because they are afraid their child may lose his spot on the team if they do not. Instead, we should get everyone on the same bus, all going in the same direction. We should do much more to help parents see why certain behavior will help their child perform better, instead of forcing them to act through fear and reciprocity.

If your club does not provide resources for parents, ask them to. Ask them where you should go to find advice on nutrition, motivation, long-term athletic development, and more. My website, www.changingthegameproject.com, has a lot of that information, and many clubs have their own advice, nutritional guidelines, and developmental curriculums. These should be easily accessible and available to parents.

Beyond this, does your club and its coaches have written core values and a mission statement they not only acknowledge but adhere to, model, and live by? Can you find this on your website? Are they in your parent handbook? Can the staff recite these values? Can the players?

When you sign up for soccer camp, they tell you your child is going to learn to dribble, pass, shoot, and head the ball. Great, easy to see what the goals of the camp are, and after the week my child should know a bit more about each of those. If you are signing your kids up for sports so they learn humility, integrity, determination, passion, and courage, is the organization preaching these values and working to teach them every day? I do not expect my child to be a better soccer player if I sign him up for basketball camp, nor should I expect him to develop strong core values if I sign him up for an organization that does not display them prominently and promise to teach them every day.

If you want your organization to change for the better, then ask for its mission statement and core values. Have them demonstrate to you how they are teaching those values and where those values place in order of importance compared to wins and losses, trophies and medals, scholarships and college commitments.

After you talk the talk, then walk the walk. Don't ask your club to change and then sit back and not be part of that change. Volunteer. Invite in guest speakers. Recommend good books or other organizations they can work with that are doing the same thing. Serve on the board of directors or head up a parent education committee to help bring this change about. There are many people quite skilled at pointing out problems. Be one of the first few that brings about solutions. Or as Gandhi stated, "Be the change that you want to see in the world."

Change Your Country

> *God, grant me the serenity to accept the things I cannot change,*
> *the courage to change the things I can, and the wisdom to know*
> *the difference.*

> **—Reinhold Niebuhr**

Positive change is like throwing a rock into calm water; you can watch the ripples spread steadily in every direction and affect everything in their path. To change youth sports, we need to throw a lot of rocks in a lot of ponds and watch the ripples spread. I know this can happen because it has happened before. Two words: Happy Meal.

McDonald's rolled out the first Happy Meal in 1979, the first kid-targeted meal with a burger, fries, soft drink, cookie, and a toy to seal the deal. There is nothing like a cheeseburger, small fries, and chocolate milk to help you cram 700 calories and 27 grams of fat into your five-year-old. But in an effort to combat childhood obesity, parents' groups in various communities have forced McDonald's to add healthier choices, such as 1% milk, salads, chicken nuggets, and apple slices. Still weighing in at 380 calories, modern Happy Meals may not be perfect, but they are better.

We will never make youth sports culture perfect, but we can make it better. If enough of us change our own actions, and change our own clubs and schools, then others will follow. Sure, Nike may still sell $250 shoes to eight-year-olds, but at least those shoes can play a part in making the kid a better person first and a better player second (To be fair to Nike, I think their "Find Your Greatness" ad in 2012, with the overweight child jogging down a lonely street, was a great first step!). At least parents can realistically decide whether a $5000 annual investment in baseball is worth Johnny becoming a confident person who can overcome any challenge he will face in life, instead of gauging the return on investment in terms of scholarship dollars.

After spending nearly two decades in youth sports, I came to realize that most parents would gladly spend hundreds on equipment or on a few hours of personal training designed to make their child stronger, quicker, and more skillful. I also realized that coaches would do almost anything to get the latest drills or best coaching techniques. Go ahead and Google "coaching drills," "speed and agility," or any sport-specific coaching advice, and you will find pages plastered with paid advertising. Why? Because people are willing to pay big money to get an edge in all of those areas.

Now go and Google "sports parenting." Not a single paid ad. Not one as of the writing of this book. Do you know why? Because people do not advertise things that do not make them money! The largest potential market in all of youth sports—helping parents make sports a positive experience for their child—is not worth a single paid advertisement because parents do not ask for help or seek advice in that area. Need to know how to run...cha-ching. Need to know how to swing...cha-ching. Need to know how to raise a confident, competent young athlete and prepare him for life by teaching him life lessons through youth sports? Crickets.

The ironic thing about this is that every new drill your child learns, or speed technique your child picks up, makes a miniscule difference on overall performance when compared to the difference you can make by nurturing a high-performing sports mindset. When you communicate well, find him a great environment, love him unconditionally, and let him go, a high performer is born. That $400 carbon fiber bat might be a bit lighter to swing, but if you want more hits, then forget the bat and make sure your child is not afraid to swing and miss. We are spending our valuable cash on the things that make the least difference and ignoring the things—many of which do not cost anything except our time—that can change everything.

When I consider why this is, I can only think of myself as a young coach. I was so afraid to show my peers and mentors that I did not know it all, so I pretended to know everything. I did not ask the right questions, for I was afraid I would seem ignorant. I did not try to learn from everyone I knew because I thought that would be perceived as a sign of weakness. And I did not prepare myself by being a student first, because I thought it was better to know a little and pretend you knew a lot than to admit I had a lot to learn and get on with learning it. As a result, many of my players and teams struggled until I learned enough to realize that I didn't know anything at all.

When I became a parent, I was determined not to repeat this mistake. I knew nothing about parenting, and I wanted to learn everything I could to try and be the best parent for my children. I asked everyone I knew who had kids. I read the books that others recommended. I got all the advice I could and then used what worked for my wife and me. I am far from perfect; I might not even be very good at all. But at least it's not for lack of effort.

When it comes to changing our youth sports culture, I believe we all need to make a greater effort to make a difference. For some people it might be to write a book or give speeches or make videos. For parents of older children who have been through the ringer once or twice, it's about passing on your knowledge to the parents of the youngest kids, perhaps through a collection of exit letters to hand to the next generation.

I recognize that it is difficult to be the first to adapt a new belief system, and that it can be difficult to stand up for what you believe when others around you exhibit destructive behavior. I get asked all the time

"How do we do this if the other team parents are not?" The answer: just do it.

Chances are good that sometime in your child's life, he or she will have friends that smoke or drink or do drugs or drive too fast. Chances are your child will have friends whose parents are not the type of role models you want your child around, and they do not exhibit the behavior you expect from other adults. At these times you will take a stand regardless of what the other parents do, because you know what you value and you know that it is the right thing for your child. Well, when it comes to sports, I see no difference. If you truly believe in something, and you are convinced that it is teaching the wrong values, you have the obligation to take a stand for what is right, regardless of who joins you.

When you make this decision, ask your sports organization to educate the membership on creating a positive and high-performing environment for our young athletes. Ask them to post core values and live by them at home and on the athletic field. Volunteer and do your part to make your organizations better, instead of looking for greener pastures. And finally, be grateful each and every day for all the amazing things in your life, for your beautiful children, and for the opportunity to make a difference.

"I have been impressed with the urgency of doing," said Leonardo da Vinci. "Knowing is not enough; we must apply. Being willing is not enough, we must do." If you have gotten this far, you have been presented with a wealth of information, but information is not knowledge. Knowledge is action, knowledge is doing. The only way you can effect a positive change is by doing something. It all starts with a small step, like a mother bird giving her chick a nudge out of the nest. She knows the chick is ready—it just needs a small push to fly.

You are now prepared to fly. You have the tools to make a difference, to change those nearest to you, and thus to change the world. Slowly but surely you will see a difference as your action ripples across your family, your team, and your community. Your change will perpetuate further change and more positive action. Youth sport will be returned to its rightful owners, our children. In the process, we will not only allow for but guide our children toward high performance. With a new sports paradigm, athletes with a high-performing state of mind, and a wave of positive change, we can become the revolution that is sorely needed by our children and by our country.

Forget about flying. It's time to soar!

7 See Rick Wolff, *The Sports Parenting Edge* (Philadelphia: Running Press, 2003). Wolff also has written numerous articles for *Sports Illustrated* on sports parenting and is the founder of The Center for Sports Parenting (www.sportsparenting.org.)

8 See Mark Hyman, *The Most Expensive Game in Town* (Boston: Beacon Press, 2012). Hyman was very gracious in answering my questions and forthcoming about the state of American youth sports. He is also author of *Until it Hurts*, about overuse injuries in youth athletics.

9 The work of Csikszentmihalyi is referenced in Daniel H. Pink's *Drive: The Surprising Truth About What Motivates Us* (New York: Riverhead Books, 2009). Though this is a business book, it gets to the heart of what motivates us to act and perform, namely autonomy, mastery, and purpose.

10 Dr. Jim Taylor, *Positive Pushing*, 105.

11 U.S. Skiing and USA Swimming have created a great resource called "Successful Sports Parenting," which is a DVD and resource materials that encompass many aspects of nutrition, development, parenting, and more. The information here was based upon one of the articles, "A Commonsense Approach to Some Challenging Issues," which was in large part based upon the national Association for Sport and Physical Education's book *Parents' Complete Guide to Youth Sports* (1989).

12 Excerpted from Dr. Jim Taylor, "The Making of a Champion" Huffington Post, June 26, 2011.

13 For a fantastic analysis of the role of genes in athletic performance, see www.sportscientists.com. Drs. Ross Tucker and Jonathan Dugas refute the notion put forth in books such as *The Talent Code*, *Bounce*, and *Outliers* by arguing that simply training and motivation do not make for elite athletic performance. They argue that culture, training, diet, and opportunity are all crucial to producing sporting champions or elite performances, but that genetics plays a role as well and should

Notes

1 See Carol S. Dweck, *Mindset: The New Psychology of Success* (New York: Ballantine Books, 2006). In my opinion, every coach, teacher, parent, and leader should own this book!

2 Paul Tough, *How Children Succeed: Grit, Curiosity, and the Hidden Power of Character* (New York: Houghton Mifflin Harcourt, 2012).

3 For more from Dan Gould, see http://www.educ.msu.edu/ysi/

4 For more information on the obesity epidemic, go to www.cdc.gov/obesity/data/adult.html

5 Uhls, Yalda and Patricia Greenfield, "The Rise of Fame: An Historical Content Analysis." *Cyberpsychology: Journal of Psychosocial Research in Cyberspace.* 5 (1), article 1, 2011. http://www.cyberpsychology.eu/view.php?cisloclanku=2011061601&article=1

6 Dr. Jim Taylor is a nationally known author and authority on parenting. His books include *Positive Pushing* and *Your Children Are Listening: Nine Messages They Need to Hear from You.* He also publishes a number of articles on the Huffington Post (http://www.huffingtonpost.com/dr-jim-taylor/), many of which I referenced in writing this book. Dr. Taylor was kind enough to speak to me and answer some of the questions I had about his work with U.S. Ski team athletes.

They provide financial assistance to help youth from low-income families, youth that are physically or developmentally challenged, and kids that are "at-risk" gain access to sports programs. They raise awareness of the importance of athletics in developing future leaders with skills and values that transfer from the sports field into the classroom, workplace, family, and community. Thank you for helping to support this great cause.

About the Author

JOHN O'SULLIVAN is the founder of the Changing the Game Project, and for the past two decades has been a successful soccer coach on the youth, high school, and collegiate level. He is a former NCAA Division I soccer player and played professionally for the Wilmington Hammerheads of the USL. John speaks nationwide to coaches, parents, and students about developing athletic excellence and leadership within positive sporting environments. He is a 1994 graduate of Fordham University and received his master's degree from the University of Vermont in 2003. He holds an "A" License from the US Soccer Federation, a National Youth Coaching License from US Youth Soccer, and currently coaches for the Portland Timbers Youth Academy of Major League Soccer.

John O'Sullivan donates a portion of the proceeds for every book sold to KIDS In The GAME. KIDS In The GAME is a 501(c)(3) nonprofit organization focused on inspiring kids to thrive in life through sports.

I need to thank Dr. Albert Oppedisano, Dr. Dan Saferstein, Dr. Jim Taylor, Mark Hyman, Bruce Brown, John Ballantine, Brian Grossman, Eric Plantenberg, Landon Johnson, and especially my brother Desmond O'Sullivan and mother Kathleen O'Sullivan for their advice, input, and editing of the many drafts of my manuscript.

Thank you to the coaches, teachers, and athletes I have played for, played with, worked alongside, and been educated by throughout the last three decades. They have given me a love of sports and a passion for learning and have taught me that coaching is about developing better people above all else. They are, in no particular order: Tom Breit, Frank Schnur, Bob Armstrong, Roby Young, Gene Buonaiuto, Bill Payoski, Al Pastore, Jerry Yeagley, Roy Patton, Roberto Beall, Ryan Levesque, Declan McSheffrey, Chris Armas, Br. Gary Cregan, Br. Jeff Pederson, Fr. Joseph McShane, Fr. Richard Dillon, Bob Jenkins, Dave Saward, Brendon Burchard, Dr. Mark Stoller, Dr. Jonathon Huener, Mike Gilligan, Felix McGrath, Tim Schulz, Don Gemmell, Brett Jacobs, and Darren Pitfield.

Finally, I need to thank the greatest coach I ever had, my father Desmond O'Sullivan, who taught me that persistence, passion, love, and integrity are the foundational values upon which any great coach, loving husband, and devoted father is built. Thanks, Dad, for everything.

Acknowledgments

WRITING A BOOK REQUIRES the input, love, and support of so many people. Writing a book that is a compilation of all you have learned in your adult life requires an exponential amount of said input, love, and support. That said, I will do my best to acknowledge everyone.

First, to my wife Lauren, who gave me the courage to take the first step, leave the full-time coaching business, and embark upon the journey to write this book and spread the message of the Changing the Game Project full-time.

Second, to my beautiful kids Maggie and Tiernan, who inspired me to write this, and while I wrote spent many hours entertaining themselves instead of playing with dad. I hope you will forgive me, and I promise that I will always play with you more in the backyard than you ever spend playing organized sports.

To David Hancock, Margo Toulouse, Jim Howard, Rick Frishman, and everyone else at Morgan James Publishing who has made this experience an incredible one.

I owe an incredible debt to my editor, Amanda Rooker, whose insight, excellence, and perceptiveness made this a much better book than it would have been if I was left to my own devices.

not be dismissed. Ultimately, their main point is that saying success is determined by only one or two things is wrong.

[14] For a fascinating dissection of the claims of Ericsson, Coyle, Syed, and Gladwell that ten thousand hours of deliberate practice is the determinant of success, go to http://www.sportsscientists. com/2011/08/talent-training-and-performance-secrets.html. Drs. Tucker and Dugas show the inaccuracies in their claims and point to other factors such as environment, genes, and more. Be sure to read the comments section, as some of the world's foremost authorities on sports performance chime in.

[15] The full LTAD program can be found on the website of The Canadian Sport For Life Foundation, www.canadiansportforlife.ca, if you would like more information.

[16] Aaron Cannon and Albert Oppedisano, *Education and Empowerment for the 21st Century Parent* (CreateSpace, forthcoming).

[17] See Cannon and Oppedisano, *Education and Empowerment for the 21st Century Parent.*

[18] Taylor, *Positive Pushing*, 80-85.

[19] You can find all of Bruce Brown's fantastic DVDs, books and more at www.proactivecoaching.info. I highly recommend his DVD "The Role of Parents in Athletics," which was required viewing for many of the teams I coached.

[20] Taylor, *Positive Pushing*, 37-40.

[21] See Taylor, *Positive Pushing*. Also referenced is an interview with Dr. Taylor conducted by Ivanhoe.com.

[22] Brendon Burchard, *The Charge: Activating the 10 Human Drives That Make You Feel Alive* (New York: Free Press, 2012).

[23] Taylor, *Positive Pushing*, 6-20.

[24] Mary Anne Radmacher is an artist and inspirational author. You can find her artwork, with quotes such as this one, at www. maryanneradmacher.net.

[25] Taylor, *Positive Pushing*.

[26] Taken from an article from the American Youth Soccer Association found at http://www.ayso.org/coaches_referees/coaches/delight_of_coaching.aspx.

Resources and Suggested Reading

Baxter, Brian. *The Sports Mindset Gameplan*. Portland, SPINw, 2012.

Brown, Bruce. "Playing with Confidence." Seattle: Proactive Coaching, 2010.

—————. *Teaching Character through Sport: Developing a Positive Coaching Legacy*. Monterey, CA: Coaches Choice, 2003.

Burchard, Brendon. *The Charge*. New York: Free Press, 2012.

Colvin, Geoff. *Talent Is Overrated*. New York: Penguin Books, 2008.

Covey, Stephen R. *The 7 Habits of Highly Effective People*. New York: Simon & Schuster, 1989.

Coyle, Dan. *The Talent Code*. New York: Bantam Books, 2009.

Dweck, Carol S. *Mindset: The New Psychology of Success*. New York: Ballantine Books, 2006.

Dyer, Wayne W. *The Power of Intention: Learning to Co-create Your World Your Way*. Carlsbad, CA: Hay House, 2004.

Gladwell, Malcolm. *Outliers: The Story of Success*. New York: Little, Brown and Co., 2008.

Goold, Derek. "Matheny's 'Manifesto' Changes Tone of Youth Baseball." *St. Louis Post Dispatch*, September 24, 2012.

Fish, Joel and Susan Magee. *101 Ways to Be a Terrific Sports Parent*. New York: Touchstone, 2003.

Hancock, Dr. Lee and Robin Russell. *Potentialing Your Child in Soccer*. Los Angeles: Hancock and Russell, 2012.

Hyman, Mark. *The Most Expensive Game in Town*. Boston: Beacon Press, 2012.

Lewis, Michael. *Coach: Lessons on the Game of Life.* New York: W.W. Norton & Co., 2005.

Philips, Donald T., Peter M. Leddy, and Rudy Ruettiger. *The Rudy in You: A Guide to Building Teamwork, Fair Play, and Good Sportsmanship for Young Athletes, Parents, and Coaches.* New York: iUniverse Satr, 2005.

Pink, Daniel. *Drive: The Surprising Truth about What Motivates Us.* New York: Riverhead Books, 2009.

Poole, Oliver. "Why We Are the Best." http://www.standard.co.uk/olympics/olympic-news/why-were-the-best-6429916.html, August 5, 2011.

Saferstein, Dan. *Strength in You: A Student Athlete's Guide to Competition and Life.* Ann Arbor, MI: Trusted Guide Press, 2006.

———. *Win or Lose: A Guide to Sports Parenting.* Ann Arbor, MI: Trusted Guide Press, 2005.

———. *Your Coaching Legacy.* Ann Arbor, MI: Trusted Guide Press, 2012.

Sax, Leonard. *Boys Adrift: The Five Factors Driving the Growing Epidemic of Unmotivated Boys and Underachieving Young Men.* New York: Basic Books, 2007.

Smoll, Frank and Robert E. Smith. *Parenting Young Athletes: Developing Champions in Sports and Life.* New York: Rowman & Littlefield Publishers, 2012.

Taylor, Dr. Jim. *Positive Pushing: How to Raise a Successful and Happy Child.* New York: Hyperion, 2003.

———. "The Making of a Champion." Huffington Post, June 26, 2011

———. "Build Athletic Confidence." Huffington Post, September 27, 2011.

Tough, Paul. *How Children Succeed: Grit, Curiosity, and the Hidden Power of Character.* Boston: Houghton Mifflin Harcourt, 2012.

———. "What if the Secret to Success is Failure?" *NY Times*, September 14, 2011.

Tucker, Ross and Jonathon Dugas. "Genes and Performances: Why Some Are More Equal Than Others." http://www.sportsscientists. com/2011/08/training-talent-10000-hours-and-genes.html#disqus_ thread, August 11, 2011.

———. "Genes vs. Training: The Secrets of Success." http://www. sportsscientists.com/2011/08/talent-training-and-performance-secrets.html, August 9, 2011.

———. "Long-Term Athlete Development: Foundations and Challenges for Coaches, Scientists and Policy-makers." http://www. sportsscientists.com/2013/02/long-term-athlete-development.html, February 12, 2013.

Uhls, Yalda and Patricia Greenfield. "The Rise of Fame: An Historical Content Analysis." *Cyberpsychology: Journal of Psychosocial Research in Cyberspace* 5, no. 1 (2011), article 1. http://www.cyberpsychology. eu/view.php?cisloclanku=2011061601&article=1, January 10, 2013.

Wolff, Rick. *The Sports Parenting Edge*. Philadelphia: Running Press, 2003.

Helpful Web Resources

Canadian Sport for Life: www.canadiansportforlife.ca
The Science of Sport: www.sportsscientists.com

Sports Parenting Resources

www.changingthegameproject.com
www.sports-parenting.com
www.responsiblesports.com
http://www.huffingtonpost.com/dr-jim-taylor/
http://www.educ.msu.edu/ysi/ (Michigan State University Youth Sports Institute)
www.positivecoach.org (Positive Coaching Alliance)
www.proactivecoaching.info (Proactive Coaching)

Join the
Changing the Game
Project Online

Join our online community at www.changingthegameproject.com and receive our latest blog posts, as well as access a wealth of information and discussions on parenting, coaching, nutrition, health and fitness, college athletics, and more.

Go there today to receive your free videos on Changing the Game and check out our numerous other products including:

- DVDs
- Podcasts
- Books
- Recommended reading list
- College recruiting tips and tricks
- And more!

Also, join our mailing list and keep up to date on speaking engagements in your area, or better yet, contact us and arrange to have John O'Sullivan come to your club or school!

We can be reached at:

changingthegameproject@gmail.com

541-977-5494

CPSIA information can be obtained
at www.ICGtesting.com
Printed in the USA
LVOW12s0023160517
534662LV00001B/116/P